Don't Do.
DELEGATE!

Don't Do. DELEGATE!

The Secret Power of Successful Managers

James M. Jenks & John M. Kelly

Kogan
Page

First published in the United States of America
in 1985 by Franklin Watts, New York

Copyright © James M Jenks and John M Kelly 1985

This edition first published in Great Britain
in 1986 by Kogan Page Ltd, 120 Pentonville Road,
London N1 9JN

British Library Cataloguing in Publication Data

Jenks, James M.
    Don't do. Delegate! : the secret power
    of successful managers
    1. Delegation of authority
    I. Title   II. Kelly, John M
    658.4'02   HD50

    ISBN 1-85091-190-8 Hb
    ISBN 1-85091-191-6 Pb

Printed and bound in Great Britain by
Billing & Sons Limited, Worcester

Contents

Introduction

This book is a definitive work on the most important skill in the successful manager's repertoire. It may also be one of the most effective tools for career advancement that any manager will encounter.

All managers face a paradox: they need to produce results beyond their individual capabilities. Finding the solution to this paradox is the key to management success. This book proves that the solution is not to *do* more, but to *delegate* more.

The unique approach of this book is to discuss delegation not as an end in itself, not as a management prerogative, not as an empty ritual of administration, but as a tool for achieving results. Delegation is treated as a goal-oriented technique. The manager is encouraged to ask: 'What results am I seeking? How can I use delegation to achieve them?'

Far from being an academic treatise on a theoretical subject, this book plunges the reader into the exciting world of expanded results. He or she will immediately begin to apply creative and proven techniques for expanding productivity and breaking through personal limitations. The book does not show the manager how to work at 100 per cent efficiency. Instead, it points the way towards achievements that are 200, 300, even 500 per cent of what any one person can accomplish alone.

Today, every company is attempting to increase productivity. The building blocks are its managers — from shop foremen to chairmen of the board. But the mortar that holds them together, that makes productivity increases a reality, is delegation.

Participation is another idea with which many companies are currently grappling. Few have yet reconciled the concept

9

with increased efficiency and results. Delegation puts participation to work. It gives a whole new meaning to goal setting, distributed decision making, even performance evaluation.

Some managers consider their 60-hour weeks and bulging briefcases they take home every night to be signs of success. The truth is that these managers are actually 'doers'. Lacking the ability to pass on tasks to their subordinates effectively, they end up 'doing' when they should be managing.

Delegating managers, on the other hand, managers who carefully apply the principles clearly laid out in this book, are not marked by their long hours or frenzied activity. Rather, they are distinguished by the one thing that really counts in any business — results. They are also distinguished by their foresight — because delegation gives them the power to plan. They are marked by flexibility — because delegation frees them from the web of petty details. And they are ultimately recognised by their personal power — because delegation allows them to accomplish through others much more than they could ever achieve individually.

This book asks every manager to pose himself or herself a question: 'If I'm having trouble delegating to my people now, how will I operate when I've been promoted to a level where even more managing and less "doing" is called for?' And it suggests the answer that every manager must face: 'If you don't learn how to delegate effectively, you'll never find out, because you'll never be promoted.'

Chapter 1

What is Delegation?

All managers face a paradox: their career advancement depends on producing results that are beyond their capabilities. Some respond by becoming workaholics. Some break down under the stress. Some turn into paper-shuffling bureaucrats. And some succeed. By doing so, they climb steadily up the corporate ladder.

What separates management winners from management losers? What secret enables successful managers to meet great expectations with limited resources? What tool virtually defines the successful manager? It is the ability to delegate.

You've encountered this paradox already. You've seen it played out around you. You've probably already realised that what distinguishes the fast-track manager is the ability to accomplish results through others. The purpose of this book is to show you the why, what, who, and how of delegating. It will guide you around the pitfalls and toward the opportunities that can mean so much to your career.

Let's look at two managers and see what an ability to delegate really can mean. As you read through this scenario, ask yourself, 'Does this sound familiar? Which type of manager am I? Which type do I want to be?'

Management of the electrical products company where Ted Murray and Bill Henderson worked promoted both to departmental supervisor at the same time. Each was considered a bright and diligent worker with good managerial promise. Each saw his promotion as the first step up the corporate ladder. However, both Ted and Bill found running a department to be a different ball game from just working in one. Their first months on the job saw them burning the midnight oil trying to keep up with the unfamiliar workload. Suddenly, they found that four or five 'crucial' problems called out for remedies all at once, that paperwork multiplied overnight, and that time had become a resource as valuable, and as scarce, as gold.

Gradually, both new managers learned to cope with the demands of their jobs. A year later, though, their paths began to diverge. Ted Murray was promoted to assistant plant manager to be groomed to succeed his boss. Bill Henderson remained a department head. What quality separated these two managers? No one argued that Bill was anything less than capable. He certainly worked hard. He knew his job thoroughly. He made no major blunders. Yet executives who observed each man at work noticed a subtle difference. Ted always seemed one step ahead of events, while Bill tended to be half a step behind. Ted's department not only completed its functions efficiently, but had become a source of innovation and extra effort. Conversely, Bill's unit was always straining to keep up with its workload. Two of Ted's people had already received promotions, while Bill's subordinates never seemed to look beyond their monthly pay cheques.

The key difference between Ted and Bill was summed up in a remark in Ted's performance evaluation: 'Knows how to delegate.' His department's more efficient operation, better planning, higher morale, and better record for developing managers could all be traced to this one talent. So could his promotion. Ted had learned how to delegate. Bill had not.

The key management skill

How could an ability to delegate make such a difference? Because delegation is the most important of all managerial skills. It is, in fact, the skill that defines a manager. A manager is someone who gets things done through people. Delegation is nothing more than accomplishing results through the efforts of others. It is the manager's most basic and important tool.

To delegate is to entrust your powers or functions to another person, to enlist that person to complete tasks that you would otherwise have undertaken yourself. You delegate when you ask your secretary to draft a reply to a routine enquiry. You delegate when you assign your assistant to handle the bulk of your duties when you're away on vacation.

Delegation is more than just assigning work. It always means making your subordinate accountable for results. It usually means giving that person the latitude to make decisions about the ways to reach those results. That's not to say that to delegate is to dump a job in your subordinate's lap and walk away. You always monitor and control the tasks you delegate. You must do this because you cannot shed the ultimate responsibility for their completion.

A delegated task is one for which you pass specific responsibility to a subordinate. Naturally, subordinates also complete the essentials of their own jobs, without much contact with you. And you yourself have a number of duties that you must always handle personally. Delegation covers the large group of tasks between these two areas, those duties that you could handle yourself, but choose to pass on to subordinates.

Delegation is always a tool, never an end in itself. Your success in delegation will never be measured by how you go about delegating, to whom you delegate, or how often you delegate. Rather, you will always be judged according to the results you achieve through delegation. Effective delegating will not just add to your achievements, but multiply them. Absence of delegation will not just slow down your career advancement in management but will inevitably stop it dead in its tracks.

Don't do — delegate

About six months after Bill and Ted were promoted, management asked all department supervisors to prepare reports on inventory control. The task involved a survey of the inventory stored in their departments, as well as an overview of internal transportation and requisition systems.

When Bill received the request, he conscientiously set about conducting the survey. Ted, on the other hand, immediately sat down to decide to whom to delegate the task. He knew that he had three subordinates who could do that job nearly as well as he could do it himself. He also figured that the research required by the report would give the person he chose a broader, more complete view of the department. He selected the person, made the assignment, and kept track of how the work progressed.

13

Why is Ted's approach better than Bill's? Bill spends the next day and a half 'doing'; that is, gathering the facts for the inventory report, tabulating figures, analysing the situation, and writing the report. Ted spends the same time 'managing'. He supervises from a distance the work of the delegatee he has selected to prepare the inventory report. At the same time he oversees other tasks that he's delegated. He plans and prepares the work of his department, keeping at least a step ahead of events. And he works on a long-range idea that he thinks will make more productive his sector of the company.

What has each manager achieved at the end of the period? Bill has produced a competent report on inventory. Ted, through the efforts of his subordinate, has done the same. But Ted has done more, has made progress in managing — planning, organising, directing, and coordinating — while Bill, if anything, has fallen behind the work of his department, has lost that half step that management had noticed. In addition, Ted has given one of his people broader experience, making that person more capable. The difference, then, is in results. Delegation has enhanced Ted's output, and lack of delegation has cramped Bill's.

Some managers have a hard time grasping this crucial distinction between 'doing' and 'managing'. Both Ted and Bill had originally been promoted because they had 'done' their jobs well. But when they entered the arena of management, even at the lowest rung, they needed to give up 'doing' to a large extent. They needed to concentrate on managing, delegating the 'doing' to their subordinates. The manager who remains a 'doer' rather than a delegator can expect little advancement.

Two key concepts in delegation

Responsibility

Delegation is a process of passing on responsibility, yet delegation never relieves you of responsibility. Some managers have a hard time reconciling these two facts. But a clear understanding of them is essential to success at delegating.

Passing on responsibility means making your subordinate accountable to you for results. You should never delegate casually. You should never convey the attitude 'if you feel like it' or 'when you get around to it'. Instead, you should agree with the delegatee on the goals to be aimed at, then insist that the person complete the task to the best of his or her ability. On time. You should emphasise that you want solutions, not problems; results, not excuses.

At the same time, you must recognise that delegation is a method of fulfilling your responsibilities, not avoiding them. You are accountable to your boss, if not directly for a specific task, then indirectly for the accomplishment of your job duties. You want your subordinates to bring you answers and achievements — your boss wants the same from you. You can't point to your delegatee and tell your boss that it's not your fault a task was botched. You are responsible.

The responsibility that goes with delegation is the same responsibility that goes with managing. It's not a light burden. It's not a burden that you can put down and take up at will. But that should never deter you from delegating. Rather, it should make you a careful delegator. Following the techniques described in this book and exercising proper controls allow you to fulfil your responsibilities without losing the myriad advantages of delegating.

Authority

'Delegation of authority' is a common, but not comprehensive, term. Authority is a resource that you make available to your subordinate. For example, in the case mentioned above, Ted had to give his delegatee the authority to elicit inventory information from the various foremen in his department. In other delegations you might have to pass along the authority to spend money, or to give orders, or to make use of company property.

Delegation should pay attention to, but not focus on, authority. Naturally, you will want to make sure that your delegatee has the authority and the other resources needed to complete the task. But delegation is not a power play, not a question of a subordinate setting up a fiefdom. Always keep the focus where it belongs — on results.

Three steps to becoming a delegator

Delegating is a skill that you learn, not a talent that you're

15

born with. Any manager who makes the effort can acquire this skill. Managers who realise the importance of effective delegation in furthering their careers make the effort. You can start on the road to becoming both a better delegator and a better manager by taking these three steps:

Attitude

No one who doesn't want to be a manager will ever become a good one. The engineer, the lawyer, the accountant — whose skills lie in the technical, rather than the interpersonal, sphere — can enjoy a successful and fruitful career without ever becoming a manager. But the person whose job is not 'doing' but getting others to do must have the desire to accomplish goals through others. If you're that kind of person, delegation is a vital tool.

Starting with the desire to be a manager, you must also want to be an achiever. The achieving manager pays attention to, but is not hypnotised by, the details of corporate organisation and administration. The achieving manager is oriented towards goals, not structures. The achieving manager takes calculated risks to expand his or her accomplishments and power. Managers who are primarily bureaucrats or paper-shufflers lack the attitude that is conducive to effective delegation.

The third important component of your attitude lies in your view of your subordinates. Effective delegators aren't autocrats or power managers. They don't look on their people as competitors, as 'the enemy'. Rather, they see their subordinates as resources for achieving results. They help them make good use of their talents, and treat them well. They don't exploit people, but help them to extend themselves. They don't confront their subordinates, but collaborate with them. They don't climb on the backs of others, but direct their efforts to raise everyone to higher levels of results.

Habit

Just knowing how to delegate won't make you an effective delegator. The person who reads the touring pros' books about how to play golf, who memorises all the relevant tips but doesn't actually swing a club, performs no better than

16

the worst duffer when he first strides on to the links. A golf swing, whether flat like Trevino's or looping like Palmer's, is largely a habit developed through long hours of practice. Theory can help to correct a slice. But only practice can assure that that theory is translated into belting the long ball down the centre of the fairway.

The only way to develop your delegating skills, the only way to become a delegator, is to delegate. Bill Henderson may have known just as much about the theory of delegating as Ted Murray did. He may have wanted just as badly to achieve the results that delegation put within Ted's reach. But he failed because he never developed the delegation habit.

Keep in mind that Ted didn't start out as a delegator either. But early in his management career he deliberately formed a habit of delegating whenever he could. He didn't succeed every time, but he persevered. His delegating skills grew. Delegation became almost automatic for him. Old habits are comfortable. New habits can only be developed with effort. However, if you don't force yourself to delegate, new achievements will be impossible.

Techniques

Later chapters in this book discuss selecting the delegatee, choosing the right tasks to delegate, making the assignment, and following up on the delegation. These techniques help to make your efforts at delegation successful and steer you away from common pitfalls. They are important because delegating is not an 'instinctive' skill. Managers tend to be dynamic and involved. Delegation requires you to step back and give your subordinate room to work. Managers like to make decisions. Delegation means transferring some of your decision making to others.

Delegation, though, is not a mechanical process. Techniques need to be fitted to the complexities of every situation and to the variables represented by the people involved — you, your subordinate, your boss, and everyone else affected by the delegation. That's why delegation is much more of an art than a science. The techniques of delegating are guidelines rather than strict rules.

Delegation and controls

Controls are among the most important techniques of effective delegation. On the surface, this seems like a contradiction. Doesn't delegating mean giving up control? Isn't the whole point to let subordinates handle tasks on their own, make decisions independently? How can you, as a manager, control without either doing the job yourself or breathing down the neck of your subordinate to see that it's done right?

The fact is that delegation never means relinquishing control. Should you delegate without adequate follow-up, you're failing as a manager. As you learn about delegation, you must also learn about getting feedback from delegatees, setting standards for them, guiding and correcting their actions to prevent disasters.

Actually, controls enhance the process of delegation in several ways. They give delegators the confidence to give up the actual 'doing' to a subordinate. Most conscientious managers feel some trepidation at letting a subordinate carry the ball for a task. Controls free them from such fears, let them yield the accomplishments without giving up the responsibilities.

Nor do controls cramp the delegatees' styles. Well-designed control systems guide them towards results, flatten hurdles, fill in potholes. Rather than stifling initiative, controls prevent them from making the kinds of serious error that can easily demoralise people attempting to venture into new areas, to learn a new skill.

Every manager's choice

The case of Ted Murray and Bill Henderson is more than just a convenient example for a book on delegation. You need not look too far to find these two types of manager. They're all around you. The Ted Murrays are found on the fast track. They get things done. They don't necessarily put in 16-hour days, carry home bulging briefcases, or scamper around in a whirlwind of frantic activity. They simply turn in consistently better results than their colleagues who haven't acquired the delegation habit. The Bill Hendersons, on the other hand, are found in the ruts of the wheel spinners, for all their honest efforts. Their output shows it; their career progress shows it.

To delegate, or not to delegate. Every manager must choose his or her own path. But experience has shown that, when it comes to management success, the delegator's path turns into the high road to success.

Chapter 2

Why Delegate?

Why delegate? It's a good question to ask.

You have to understand the reasons for delegation in order to develop effective approaches to it. Delegation is not a formality, not an exercise that can be learned by rote, not a peripheral aspect of the real job of managing. Delegation is the essence of managing. Neither you nor anyone else can be a good manager without being a good delegator.

To understand why you must delegate, and delegate effectively, you have to know what results you are trying to achieve, your goals and objectives, and how delegation puts them within your grasp. You also will understand better the importance of delegation when you are able to spot quickly the morass of wasted effort and organisational stagnation that develops when managers delegate poorly.

The signs of poor delegation

Poor delegation is a fundamental cause of weak management. Unfortunately, though, poor delegation practices don't stand out like flashing beacons in a manager's day-to-day functioning. They're hard to put a finger on.

To answer the question, 'Why delegate?', look for the signs of poor delegation. Those signs are visible to experienced top executives just as animal tracks are to good hunters. First take a look at yourself, at how ineffective delegation may be cramping your own management style and your opportunities for advancement.

Signs close to home

- Poor delegation is sapping your time.

- Poor delegation is burying you in trivia.
- Poor delegation is causing conflicts with subordinates.

You won't need to look far to find signs of poor delegation — no farther than the tower of work in your 'in' tray, no farther than the bulging briefcase you carry home every night, and no farther than that knot in your stomach that occurs as you bump into deadline after deadline with work incomplete.

Time and trivia. Never enough time. And too much trivia. Far too much. Consider two examples:

1. The sales manager of an electrical equipment distributor needed to make the rounds of the company's six district sales offices every month. Ideally, he'd spend three days on the road, taking plenty of time to size up the situation at each office. Instead, he tried to hit all six offices in two days. If he could have cut the trip to a single day, he would have.

Why? He dreaded facing the pile of work on his desk when he returned. He hated the thought of problems snowballing while his subordinates waited for him to get back. He knew that he'd be catching up for the rest of the week after his trip.

These are classic signs of poor delegation. This manager had made himself the tightly wound mainspring of his department. He made things go. However, unlike the mainspring of a clock, which drives the wheels and gears that turn the second, minute, and hour hands, he released no power to others. He made all decisions, let nothing go. As a result, when he returned from his trips he was inundated by letters, memos, and questions from his subordinates and his boss. His time was consumed by trivia. Therefore, he had to cut back on the amount of time he should have devoted to more important tasks of managing.

2. Friday afternoon. The plant supervisor of a packaging company calls in a subordinate to ask about next month's production schedule. The subordinate apologises. He didn't realise that it had to be completed so soon. He hands over the half-finished job. The supervisor resigns himself to missing another Saturday at the links.

The supervisor delegated the task, but was unclear about

the deadline. Maybe the subordinate knew how easily he could turn work back to his boss — delegate upward. In any case, the boss ends up putting in the long hours. And contrary to popular belief, the bloodshot eyes of overwork are not the red badges of a manager's courage. They are, instead, signs of ineffective delegation.

Signs from relationships with subordinates

Too little time and too much trivia are not the only signs of poor delegation that you may find in yourself. Other signs appear in the way you relate to your subordinates. When was the last time you elicited a subordinate's opinion about a work assignment? How much more often do you find yourself saying, 'Do this' rather than, 'How's it going?'

Delegation is an interpersonal skill. If your personal relations with subordinates are weak, then you'll have problems delegating. That doesn't mean that the good-natured, amiable manager makes the most effective delegator. It means that secretive, autocratic, distrustful, uncommunicative managers are more likely to run into delegation problems.

For example, the manager of a staff of design engineers was called in by her boss to explain why her team showed consistently lower productivity than other teams. She couldn't explain it.

Her subordinates, however, could. The manager would not tolerate the least error. Nor did she share information with them. She felt they didn't need to know. As a result, her subordinates did everything by the book. They checked their work more closely than necessary to avoid the manager's displeasure. They sometimes found themselves idle while waiting for the manager's instructions. The manager's intolerance of minor mistakes and failure to communicate useful information were signs of her inability to delegate effectively.

Signs from your people

- Your subordinates lack initiative.
- Your subordinates fail to seek your assistance, or seek it too frequently.
- Your subordinates are often dissatisfied with their jobs.

These signs of poor delegation show that it takes two to delegate. You lead, your subordinate follows. If you haven't got the rhythm, you're both going to trip up.

Initiative in your subordinates is a key sign of how well you are delegating. If you are delegating poorly, initiative will be conspicuous by its absence. Poor delegation can be like a rickshaw. You do all the pedalling. Your subordinates are along for the ride. Don't be surprised if managing is hard, gruelling work.

Take the case of a security manager in charge of a large factory complex. His shift supervisors showed no initiative. Every proposed change in guard assignments, every buying decision, every scheduling difficulty landed on his desk.

Were his people simply dull? No. He was a poor delegator. Every time shift supervisors asked him, 'What do you think?' he gave them specific answers. The please-the-boss syndrome took over and they began always to ask his opinion. Their lack of initiative should have alerted him to his own delegating deficiencies. He should have begun responding to their questions by asking, 'What do *you* think?'

When your subordinates never come to you for assistance, that's just as much a sign of poor delegation as their constant checking. Do you fail to learn about problems until subordinates are actually floundering? Do your people try to cover up difficulties they're having with assignments? Do they assure you that things are all right when they're not?

Poor delegation is often the culprit. Maybe you snatch back work at the first sign that the subordinate can't handle it. Maybe you're too quick to blame or berate a subordinate. Maybe you've forgotten that there's a learning curve for any task. All of these attitudes will be reflected in your people. They should alert you that you are not delegating effectively.

Job dissatisfaction as a sign of poor delegation

Initiative refers to how your subordinates do their jobs. Satisfaction refers to how they feel about them. The two are closely related. Lack of job satisfaction among people who work for you often signals poor delegation.

The vice president of a food processing company assigned to the marketing director an assistant to ease his workload and be trained to replace the marketing director when he was promoted. At first the assistant showed considerable aptitude. The marketing director showed his assistant the ropes and gave her plenty of work to keep her busy. After 18 months, though, the assistant asked to be transferred. She said she found no stimulation in marketing. Her boss agreed that the woman's performance had been on a plateau for some time. He approved the transfer request.

Had he been alert, the marketing director might have seen the situation as a sign that he was not delegating effectively. He had shown his assistant how things worked, he had assigned her tasks, but he had not really delegated. He'd kept her busy but had never given her complete responsibility for any of his duties. He hadn't truly delegated – had not let her learn by doing. She had become stale by doing 'busy work'. She wasn't gaining new experience each month. She was simply repeating the same experiences month after month.

How your environment signals poor delegation

- Poor delegation environments are marked by confusion.
- Poor delegation environments are stagnant.
- Communication difficulties often accompany poor delegation environments.

Patterns of poor delegation apply to organisations as well as to individuals. Again, look for the signs.

It's important to be able to recognise when you are working in an environment that is marked by poor delegation. First, you can do something to rectify the matter within your sector. Second, you're going to have a tougher time managing when you're working in an environment infected with poor delegation.

Confusion in a company often signals that managers are not effectively delegating. Lines of authority are not clear. Job assignments overlap. Responding to crises and 'putting out fires' take the place of rational planning.

For example, corporate headquarters sent out an administrative director to evaluate the firm's unprofitable transport division. The executive found high costs and low revenues because of disorganisation. The division manager had not devised clear job descriptions at any level. Some areas of responsibility overlapped. Other tasks were left to be handled by whoever took them on. Pointless meetings took the place of effective management.

Poor delegation lay under the surface in this case. Effective organisations are built on pyramids of delegations. Managers receive clear areas of responsibility from their bosses They in turn delegate certain tasks to their subordinates. Without these orderly structures, organisations fall into confusion. Results, and profits, fly out of the window.

Stagnation is another sign of poor delegation on an organisational level. Methods are emphasised over results. The organisation reacts slowly to change. Position and status become more highly valued than opportunities to be effective. The organisation has no clear priorities other than perpetuating itself. Rigidity replaces flexibility.

The New York Central Railroad fell prey to this syndrome some years ago. While many other problems beset the railroad during this time, the former director of management development said that at New York Central, managers 'retired while still behind their desks'. They continued to do the same tasks over and over and failed to delegate, causing lower morale among lower level managers and perceptions that no opportunities existed for advancement or accomplishment. The New York Central stagnated, then merged with the Pennsylvania Railroad; as the Penn Central, it finally was forced into bankruptcy.

Yet other railroads, confronting the same problems, continued to operate successfully. They rode out the same storms. They continued to provide their customers with excellent service and their shareholders with decent returns on their investments. Again, it has been reported that managing skills — delegating abilities among them — freed these railroads from the stagnating climates that felled so many others.

Poor information flow often characterises the organisation with delegating problems. Secrecy always inhibits effective delegation. Decisions are referred upstairs. Requests for information come down from above. Nobody wants to act without something in writing from the boss. A memo blizzard develops. Orders are passed down, but they aren't timely. More problems develop. The process starts over again. Poor delegation has become institutionalised.

Should you see in your own company that people are not

'getting the word', that the channels of communication are choking on memos with conflicting information, that indecision is rampant among top management executives, then blow the whistle. You'll know that the non-delegators are blocking the road to progress. Westinghouse Electric lost its consumer markets to General Electric for its failure to delegate effectively to divisional level managers. All American auto companies lost the subcompact car market to foreign manufacturers for failure to delegate responsibility and authority to eager young engineering managers, who could have beaten back the threat.

The checklist below gives common signs of poor delegation. You might want your company to acquire additional copies of this book for peers and subordinates who have tasks, duties, and jobs that are delegatable. Use the checklist to see how many of the signs of poor delegation apply directly to you, how many apply to your people, and how many apply to your organisation. Don't be afraid to plead 'guilty' to the possible charges of poor delegation. Compare your checklist with others who are reading this book for their evaluations. Remember, the first step in solving a problem is to recognise that you have one and to be able to define it precisely. This checklist, and the problem-solving sessions it will provoke among you, your colleagues, and your people, will help you all become delegators — managers who can delegate for results.

Keep referring to this list as you improve your delegating skills. Track the number of signs that you have eliminated through better delegating.

Checklist to find signs of poor delegation

You

☐ Your workload has prevented you from taking regular holidays.
☐ You feel overworked frequently.
☐ You leave jobs unfinished.
☐ Most nights and weekends you take work home.
☐ It always seems as if you have more work to do than your subordinates.

☐ Planning is a low priority task for you.

☐ You have no time for outside civic or recreational activities.

☐ In the past week, you've engaged in detailed work that is not part of your job.

☐ Frequently you end up doing your subordinates' work for them.

☐ Crises and problems are more common in your job than opportunities.

☐ Often, you haven't time to explain a task fully to your subordinate.

☐ You frequently have problems meeting deadlines.

☐ You like to keep your hand in your old job.

☐ You're a perfectionist — and proud of it.

☐ You wish you had more time to devote to your family.

☐ You can't immediately name your top three current work goals.

☐ You believe in giving subordinates only the information they need to do their specific jobs.

☐ You rarely elicit the opinions of your subordinates about anything.

☐ You issue orders very frequently.

☐ Your subordinates are not to be trusted too far, in your opinion.

☐ You feel the stick is generally more effective than the carrot.

☐ It's hard for you to accept ideas offered by someone else.

Your people

☐ You sometimes get the feeling they're trying to undermine you.

☐ They're freewheeling.

☐ How something is done is more important to them than what is achieved.

☐ They refuse to make any decisions without consulting you first.

☐ They're out of control.

☐ More frequently than necessary, they come to you for advice on their work.

☐ They exceed their authority regularly.

☐ They act according to the letter rather than the spirit of an assignment.

- Sometimes, they consult with you only after the fact about significant actions.
- None of them could fill in for you if you had to be away.
- They turn work assignments back to you and get away with it.
- They wouldn't work at all if you weren't there to push them.
- Their skills are essentially unchanged from a year ago.
- They rarely come to you with new ideas or new ways of doing their jobs.
- None of them is likely to succeed you when you leave your position.

Your organisation

- No one seems to know what's most important.
- Planning, especially long-term, is inadequate.
- Confusion frequently arises about job descriptions and areas of responsibility.
- No clear line of authority exists through the organisation.
- Decisions — even minor ones — are usually made at high levels of management.
- Important tasks are left to be handled by 'whoever'.
- Methods are emphasised over results.
- Criticism is more common than praise.
- Status arises only from position, not accomplishment.
- The operation is a one-man show and everybody knows it.
- Workaholics are favoured for promotion.
- The organisation has a low ratio of secretaries or assistants to managers.
- Controls are too tight and require too much paperwork.
- The ability to delegate effectively is not considered in performance appraisals.
- Management development is non-existent or has a low priority.
- Key managers are frequently brought in from outside the organisation.
- The organisation is slow to react to change.
- Younger managers frequently leave the firm.
- Managers are often expected to chip in on detailed work.
- Communication is limited and contained rather than extensive and widespread.
- The idea of participation is seen as soft-headed.

Positive results of delegation

You've seen how poor delegation gives rise to a host of
management ills. But other than eliminating these problems,
what does the skill of being able to delegate more effectively
offer managers?

Results-oriented delegation will improve your work situation, benefit your organisation, and help your subordinates.
And, when you become a successful delegator, you'll probably get a new 'psychological contract' from your management that will be valuable to your career. You'll gain money,
power, security. Consider the most important positive results
in each of these areas.

Delegation multiplies your productivity

Your task as a manager is to produce, to achieve results.
Like anyone else, you're strictly limited in the work you can
complete in a given amount of time. The only way you can
increase results is to get work done through others. The
most effective way to work through others is to delegate.

In the same way that gearing — borrowing money — allows
a business to produce more with the same equity capital,
so delegation magnifies the efforts of the individual manager.
For example, if you spend half an hour delegating a task to a
subordinate and he spends four hours working at the task,
then you have produced up to eight times the results you
could get had you not delegated.

Borrowing money to finance a business can be risky.
True. And delegation has its risks as well. But when you use
proven delegation techniques and control delegations successfully, those risks become insignificant compared with the
results that delegation puts within your grasp.

The improved productivity benefit of delegation is illustrated in this case: the personnel manager for a small,
growing communications equipment company needed to hire
additional engineers. The manager usually found a few top
candidates by attending 'career days' at local colleges.

Many of the colleges held these sessions at the same time
of the year. The manager could attend only half a dozen of
them. His opinion that none of his subordinates could make

these important hiring decisions limited his results in this area.

The need for new engineers, though, made him turn to delegation. He selected four of his subordinates and carefully explained to them the type of candidates the company was looking for. He versed them in interviewing techniques. Then he sent them into the field.

As a result of delegation, the company was now represented at 30 colleges instead of six. Delegation multiplied the manager's effectiveness. He kept control by screening all the potential candidates his subordinates selected.

Another interesting example of increased productivity resulting from delegation involves union members. Eastern Airlines has experienced disastrous financial losses in recent years. Productivity improvement was targeted by management and union leaders as an area to focus on to reduce costs and meet heated competition from low-cost airlines such as People Express.

With union agreement, Eastern has delegated authority to the lead ramp crew boss to clear a plane for takeoff once it has been loaded. Formerly, only a supervisor could clear the plane for takeoff. One lead ramp crew member estimated that such changes have resulted in a 30 to 40 per cent increase in productivity. Moreover, the changes have shifted responsibility to a more appropriate level, increased job satisfaction, and allowed greater management flexibility — all factors dealt with at greater length later in this chapter.

The supervisor still retains control over this delegation, however. If there are delays, the lead ramp man must report the cause to the supervisor.

Delegation gives you time

The top-notch but harried manager, desk overflowing with clutter, is a myth. The best managers find time to think and plan. Time is a manager's most valuable commodity. And delegation is the best way to free time for important managerial duties.

Consider the quality control manager at a company that manufactures automotive parts. Besides a heavy workload of formulating quality control standards and directing their

31

implementation, his time was eaten up by meetings in which his inspectors reported on problems to departmental production managers. He attended the meetings out of habit, though he rarely contributed anything.

He rid himself of this time-consuming task by delegating it to his assistant. The assistant prepared a concise weekly report listing the details of these meetings. This delegation released an extra half day each week for the manager to use for other pressing tasks.

Eliminating trivia through delegation

You're the plant superintendent. You start your day by filling in figures on the monthly production report, although all you really do is transfer the numbers supplied to you by the foreman in each department. Next, you drop around the engineering department and talk over two new products. It's not really necessary, but you think you can make some suggestions since you used to be in engineering. Then you remember that one of your subordinates asked you to put pressure on purchasing to speed up deliveries of certain parts. Next, you take a call from the phone company about a problem with one of the long distance lines. As soon as you hang up, you're off to the company library to check on the durability of a type of plastic to be used in a new product. That done, you finally have time to sit down and weigh the pros and cons of expanding the warehouse. Unfortunately, within 10 minutes you have to run off to a meeting concerning the visit next week of the company divisional director.

Trivia have stolen the morning from you. The bane of every manager, trivia may annoy you, or you may revel in them. In either case, they sap your energy and distract you from the more important aspects of your job. Trivia constantly interrupt your concentration.

When you've learned to delegate effectively, you'll turn over completion of the production report to your assistant. He may take twice as long to fill it in. You'll certainly review his work briefly the first few times. But it's one piece less of trivia. You'll stop dabbling in engineering entirely. That's no longer your job. You'll tell your subordinate to deal with purchasing himself. You'll tell your secretary to refer the phone problem to the chief of maintenance. And you'll send a subordinate to the library and a representative to the meeting. You'll then devote your entire morning to the important warehouse decision. And you'll reach a decision. Delegation will let you work toward results rather than sacrifice time to trivia.

How delegation allows you to manage

Ask yourself, 'Once I've delegated a substantial portion of my current work, what do I do with myself?' The answer: you manage.

- You *plan.* You set goals, consider contingencies, devise methods for achieving results. You look ahead.
- You *direct.* You guide subordinates towards effective efforts without making decisions for them. You check their work to keep them on track.
- You *organise.* You devise structure and policy that is best suited to maintaining efficiency within your sphere of control.

Delegation clears away time for all these important managerial tasks. It helps you to avoid crises and to cope with them when they come. It turns you from a 'doer' into a true manager.

Developing your management abilities through delegation

Practising delegation improves your ability to manage. And while delegation is important for all people who manage, it is increasingly crucial at higher levels. A foreman to some extent still does things even though he or she delegates to others. A director does much more delegating than 'doing', and should be a better delegator because of all the practice.

Because delegation is a fundamental interpersonal process, the act of delegating enhances your ability to work with others. Ordering someone to do something requires little skill. Delegating authority and responsibility to others requires adeptness in communication, a willingness to listen, a knack for motivation, and an ability to convey trust and inspire loyalty.

Delegating promotes organisational efficiency

In world trade, the law of comparative advantage holds that all nations benefit if each makes those goods that it can produce most efficiently and imports those goods that other countries can produce at lower cost. This rule applies to efficiency in organisations as well. The organisation benefits if each member concentrates on that area in which he or she has a comparative advantage.

Note that it is a comparative advantage, not an absolute advantage, that is important. An inventory manager may be an excellent typist. He can type even faster than his secretary. But his secretary has very limited skills in making inventory decisions. The rule of comparative advantage states that the organisation will benefit from the manager sticking strictly to inventory decisions and delegating all typing to his secretary.

Look at reasons for delegating by examining the best use of resources. Delegation pushes work downwards to be completed by lower-paid workers rather than higher-paid managers. More work is done for each pound paid in wages.

Take the case of a computer software firm's accountant, who was promoted to controller. His duties included managing a 12-person accounting staff.

This manager was an expert in cost accounting. He liked cost accounting and had substantial experience in the field. Costing out a typical project took him about two hours. The subordinate who would take over cost accounting was less adept and usually spent at least three hours on a project.

Would the company benefit from having the new controller pitch in and handle cost accounting? No. First, he was being paid twice the salary of his subordinate. So it cost the firm more for him to handle the projects even though he worked faster. Second, the controller could handle many managerial tasks that the subordinate could not. Delegating the cost accounting improved overall efficiency.

How delegation shifts decision making to the appropriate level

Decisions are perishable. By the time the facts about a situation are passed up through channels and a decision passed down, the situation can easily have changed.

Delegation — as opposed to simple task assignments — always requires of a subordinate a certain degree of decision making. The subordinate exercises judgement depending on the circumstances. Delegation promotes more timely, better quality decisions. The decision maker has a feel for the situation that can't always be conveyed to the boss through statistical or even oral reports. The company benefits.

A sales manager of a company selling plastic containers didn't allow his sales representatives to make any price concessions without first checking with him. But in many cases he approved the lower price for the item after reviewing the sales reps' arguments.

The market in which the company operated, though, was highly competitive. Sales reps reported the firm lost profitable accounts either because of delays caused by their seeking approval of minor price changes, or because the sales manager didn't understand the nuances of handling certain customers.

After a period of sluggish sales growth, the sales manager decided to try delegation. He told his subordinates that they could decide price alterations within certain limits for each product line. Given this flexibility, the sales reps landed additional business without significantly eroding margins. The firm's market share increased.

Why delegation facilitates decentralisation and diversification

Growth usually means spreading out geographically. It often means entering new markets or even new industries. A company with a single location and limited markets may squeeze by in spite of poor delegation. But when it begins to expand into new areas, problems develop.

A manager whose subordinates are located in the next office may get away with minimal delegating. But what if they're located in another part of the country? Can they communicate what's going on there quickly and effectively? Will his decisions be as timely as theirs would be with delegated authority? No.

For companies that practise effective delegation, de-centralisation and diversification come easily. Managers in charge of new locations are delegated the authority and decision-making power they need. They aren't encumbered by unwieldy chains of command, only guided by efficient systems of control.

Delegation supports results-oriented participation

The benefits of participatory management have been debated for a number of years. Some companies have formed special workers' committees to provide input into management decision making. Chrysler Corporation seated the head of the automobile workers' union on its board of directors.

But there is no better way than delegation to promote meaningful participation by employees in the company's operation. Having labour representatives sitting on boards of directors may increase workers' sense of involvement. But delegating to them each day tasks that give them a chance to make actual decisions makes them feel that they are more in control, that they are making contributions to specific results. For the company, this translates into greater employee satisfaction, lower overheads, better results.

Delegation increases management flexibility

A large, diversified company that emphasised effective delegation at all levels moved a young financial manager from its consumer products division to its industrial fastener subsidiary to give her a broader view of the company. At her new job she sat down with the 10 people who would be working for her. She asked each, 'What are your current goals and how are you going to achieve them?' That done, she surveyed and discussed operations with colleagues. The work of her sector proceeded. She already had a grasp of its essentials.

This example shows another benefit to the organisation of good delegation. The manager easily made the transition from one division to another because in this company, managers manage. That is, they delegate. In a firm with poor delegation, the manager would have been caught up in complicated webs of petty details and smothered by subordinates' requests for advice and decisions. The activity of her staff would have slowed until she became familiar with the many things that she would have to handle personally in the department.

This type of flexibility is invaluable for a company, particularly one that's growing. By delegating details, managers become specialists in the art of managing.

Delegation increases job satisfaction

Taking orders is tedious. Making decisions is fun. Rote assignments are boring. New challenges stimulate. Being a cog in a machine makes workers stale. Being contributors makes them enthusiastic.

A warehouse foreman at a building products firm had spent many years at his job. However, as one of his fellow foremen put it, 'He's as lazy as a turtle sunning on a sandbank.' He did his job all right, but he saved all his enthusiasm for his rugby league. His subordinates liked him, but his superiors considered him barely competent.

A new warehouse manager arrived. He called the foreman into his office to discuss improved stock handling in the warehouse. He asked if the foreman thought this was feasible. 'Certainly', the man replied. 'There are many things that can be done.' The manager laid out some of the criteria he thought should apply to the effort, then asked the foreman to come up with a plan in six weeks.

The foreman's workers were surprised to see him become a whirlwind of activity. He studied records. He talked to marketing and production managers. He read up on modern inventory management systems. 'He looks like he's working for a promotion,' one worker remarked.

During the week that the foreman worked out the details of the new stock plan, he even passed up his regular training night. 'Got more important things to do,' he told team members.

This is just one example of how a delegated task that gave the delegatee responsibility, trust, and power lifted him out of the deadly job routines and revitalised him.

Delegation provides variety and novelty

Tasks become easier as they are repeated. That's what industrial engineers call the learning curve. But tasks that are initially fascinating can also become tedious with repetition. That might be called the boredom curve.

Many managers' duties are susceptible to the boredom curve. The first few meetings, the first few reports, the first few inspection trips are invigorating. Then they become commonplace. Finally they merge into monotonous routines.

But for managers' subordinates, being entrusted with completing important reports presents novel challenges. Being asked to attend meetings as representatives of their bosses is a reward. Going out on site inspections is a welcome break from routine.

For example, the marketing director of a Philadelphia toy company attended a trade show each spring on the West Coast. Though the show wasn't a major exhibition, she felt she should go to keep an eye on competitors and to spot developing trends. Actually, she'd begun to dread the long trip and the disruption of her schedule at a time when she was especially busy.

The solution? She delegated the task to a promising assistant. It was his first business trip and he welcomed the opportunity to get out of the office. Far from being a grind, the trip stimulated him. He returned full of new ideas and bursting with enthusiasm.

Developing skills by delegation

Becoming a good delegator is a learning process as well as a way to accomplish specific results. The teacher in this process is not just the delegator but experience itself. No amount or kind of training teaches soldiers what it is like to be under fire, not even crawling through obstacle courses with instructors firing live ammunition precisely aimed to pass a foot or two overhead. Textbooks can't take the place of doing, though they can speed up the preparation for doing.

While training programmes can teach employees specific skills such as computer programming, delegation can teach subordinates a variety of general skills by doing. Decision making is a good example. Because delegation requires subordinates to make some decisions, they experience the need to gather information, weigh it carefully, and make timely choices from among available options.

You'll find it hard to teach (or to learn) self-direction without using delegation. While you may set deadlines for results, your delegatees must estimate the amount of work to be done, pace their efforts, and motivate themselves to complete the tasks. They must learn to use their own judgements. The people who always have their courses charted by their bosses get no experience in these skills.

Delegation improves evaluation of people's potential

The purpose of delegating tasks is not to test subordinates, not a question of do or die. Delegation, however, often does provide indications of delegatees' strengths and weaknesses that would not otherwise be apparent.

The labour relations manager for a large tyre company had on his staff a very bright and talented researcher. The manager planned to promote one of his people to assistant manager and was considering this young man for the position.

He decided to delegate to him a minor negotiating session with the union representatives at one of the firm's subsidiaries. He thoroughly briefed the subordinate on what to expect and sent him off. The results were not spectacular. The session left most issues still unresolved. For his part, the subordinate felt that while he enjoyed working behind the scenes, he wasn't cut out to be a face-to-face labour negotiator. The job wasn't for him.

This delegation did not produce the optimum short-term results. The manager could have attended the session himself and achieved more than his subordinate. However, it did yield important long-term results. It helped the manager to size up a subordinate based on real experience rather than assumption. It gave him clues so that he could guide the subordinate into a rewarding career path rather than one that wouldn't suit him.

Managers sometimes have difficulties evaluating subordinates. Do they decide quickly after weighing relevant facts? Do they overlook important details? Do they work well with others? Do they show initiative? Watching their performances in delegated tasks frequently answers these questions.

Chapter 3

What to Delegate?

A cartoon that recently appeared in the *New Yorker* magazine showed a manager seated in the middle of a spacious but empty office. He is explaining to a colleague: 'All I need is a chair. I delegate everything.'

This idea is not quite as absurd as it sounds. In fact, it should be your starting point when you take up the question of what to delegate. A good manager should be just as anxious to find opportunities to delegate. Don't ask, 'Why delegate?' Ask, 'Why not delegate?' If you can think of no good reason for holding on to a task, then find a way to delegate it. Delegate everything.

A sudden departure

The production control supervisor in an automobile components company asked himself a question: 'What if I had to leave today and be away from the plant for a month?'

He began to dwell on what he imagined would happen if, given a single day to arrange things, he had to leave the plant and let his job be handled by his current subordinates.

- Would the production line immediately slow down or even close down?
- Would disastrous production problems develop within a few days?
- Were his people ready to fill in for him?
- Would the company lose business or profit? How much?
- Would operations in fact run quite smoothly with only minor snags?

He drew up a list of the major tasks that confronted him in

the coming months. Then he briefly noted the best people to handle each duty. He tried to imagine how well they would get the jobs done, what kind of instructions they'd need, what additional authority he'd have to give them.

Some tasks clearly could not be handled properly by the subordinates. Hiring and firing decisions, salary recommendations, budget variances, and long-term production plans all required his personal attention. But most of these tasks could easily await his return without throwing a monkey wrench into day-to-day operations.

The manager foresaw few problems. He'd delegated tasks in the past and had a good idea of the capabilities of his staff. He'd have a pile of work waiting for him when he got back, but his month away would hardly bring the company to a grinding halt. As a result of his speculation, the manager decided to take a two-week holiday, his first in several years.

You're leaving today

You can benefit from a similar analysis. Take a close look at everything you do in a month. Then imagine being called away on short notice. Ask three questions about each task:

- Who among your subordinates could take care of it?
- What authority and preparation would the person need?
- How good a job would the person do?

Once you have done this, examine each task that could be adequately handled by one of your subordinates with no more than moderate preparation. Now ask, 'Why am I not delegating this task to him or her now?'

Don't pretend this is an easy question. Pat answers like, 'I've always done it myself,' or, 'I like doing it,' or, 'It looks better if I handle it personally' won't hold water. You are trying to break through into new patterns that are more effective than the way you've 'always done it'. Nor does a good manager spend time doing work that could be delegated just because such work is pleasant. And as far as appearances go, improved results always look better than feverish activity, or always scrambling like a cat on a hot tin roof.

If you think that some task is not part of the subordinate's job, then why isn't it? Couldn't it be added to that person's duties?

If you argue that the subordinate would take longer than you do to finish the task, remember the law of comparative advantage. Shifting work downward benefits the organisation even if a particular task is not accomplished as quickly. Consider also the learning curve. Your subordinate, in time, may become as adept at completing a job as you are.

But the object of this exercise is not to give you time off for a month's holiday. It is to identify areas of your current responsibility that you could delegate. Don't resist giving up tasks. Try to delegate everything. If you can't picture yourself as the man in the *New Yorker* cartoon who delegated so well that all he needed to perform his job was a chair, then imagine yourself at least able to clear off your desktop by the end of each week.

Make yourself dispensable

Like many managers, you may have a common but mistaken notion of your job. You want to be indispensable to your organisation. If the company can't survive without you, you feel secure. You're appreciated. You have a degree of power. You're valuable. And wanted.

But you also feel you must work to stay indispensable. You are reluctant to give up any task, however trivial. You have a finger in every pie.

Take the case of a set-up man in the machine shop of an aircraft manufacturer. He excelled at his job and the company soon promoted him to foreman. One of the machines in his department was especially complicated. It needed expert maintenance during any changeover. This man had worked with the machine for so long that he knew where to find the gremlins when they caused mechanical troubles in it. It was his 'baby'. Whenever a problem arose, he stepped in to handle it personally.

Was this man indispensable? In his mind the answer was 'yes'. But his company was paying a foreman's salary to have work done that should and could have been taken care of by a lower-paid worker. And the foreman was damaging his own chances for promotion. How could he move out of the department to a higher level job if no one could take over who had experience on this machine? The foreman had tossed out an anchor that was certain to be a drag on his future upward career movement.

A better goal is to make yourself dispensable. Delegate to your people. Give them experience. Give them the information, instruction, and training they need. Get them ready to take over for you. The more you delegate, the faster you prepare for the day when you really do turn over your entire job to a successor and move up a step in the organisation.

Doing versus delegating

Every manager's duties can be divided into three levels:

Doing

This means directly accomplishing results. It includes operating a machine or pushing a broom. But it also covers writing a legal brief, making an engineering drawing, closing a sale, or looking into a customer complaint.

Directing

This includes tasks in which you are directly involved in supervising work. Coaching, giving instructions, overseeing completion, reviewing results, and holding meetings are all aspects of directing.

Planning

Here you are not directly involved in the work but influence it from a distance. Strategic planning, laying out financial tactics, devising a marketing campaign, drawing up a budget, working out a production schedule, and mapping stock requirements are all aspects of the planning level.

Almost all managers handle tasks at each of these levels. But the higher a manager moves in the organisation, the less doing and the more planning he or she engages in. You eliminate the 'doing' aspects of your job by delegating them. The more 'doing' you can pass on to subordinates, the better you will manage and the more you will resemble the most successful managers.

Tasks to delegate

It would be convenient if you could step back from your job and neatly classify all of your current tasks, duties, and jobs according to whether or not they can potentially be delegated to subordinates. Unfortunately, a steady onslaught of distractions, complex details, and stimuli in your daily work leaves you with a much more complicated view of what you can or should delegate.

The following guidelines can help you isolate tasks that often make good candidates for delegation. Naturally, you must evaluate each task on its own merits. However, those that fall into one of these categories are worth considering:

- Routine
- Necessity
- Trivia
- Specialities
- Chores
- Pet projects.

Routine

When you do a task repeatedly, that spotlights it as one to delegate. Why? First, because a routine task is usually easy to pass on to a subordinate. You've done it yourself. You're aware of any problems that may come up. You approach it with tested methods.

Second, delegating routine pays big dividends. Once you've prepared the delegatee, set up controls, and passed on the task, you're a winner — you benefit each time the person performs it. The results you achieve from passing on routine tasks are greater than those that flow from a one-time delegation.

Consider a simple example. You arrive at your office every morning and open your mail. You sort out the junk mail, identify the high-priority items, and separate the purely information letters from those requiring future action, sending some to peers for their information and others for filing. Why couldn't you delegate this routine task? If you don't have a personal secretary, assign it to another subordinate. Explain how you would like your mail arranged. Let that person take care of it. Even if you save only 10 minutes a day, that's nearly an hour a week that you have gained to devote to more important matters, especially thinking and planning.

Take the example of an assistant magazine publisher who was responsible for approving requests to use the company's mailing lists. The firm followed a policy of only renting the lists to educational and related institutions. While such requests had been infrequent in the past, lately they had been coming in more regularly. The assistant publisher found that she now spent nearly two hours a week reviewing requests.

The woman recognised that this routine task was an obvious candidate for delegation. She explained to a secretary in her department how to divide the requests into three categories. She instructed the secretary to send to the clearly commercial enquirers a form letter explaining company policy. She should pass directly to the marketing department enquiries from educational institutions. The few uncertain cases should be turned back to the assistant publisher for a decision. By this delegation, the assistant publisher created more time for managing by eliminating some of the routine 'doing' from her job.

Necessity

While you have specific areas of responsibility, your job description does not mandate all of your tasks. You take on many discretionary duties. You do them when you know they need to be done.

As a rule, tasks that must be done — either because they are dictated by company policy or because they are necessary aspects of the manager's duties — can be more readily delegated than those that are discretionary. You can more easily define and explain mandated tasks to the delegatee. While they may involve decisions, they usually call for less managerial judgement.

Discretionary tasks, on the other hand, often call for evaluation and judgement. You bring your more diversified and higher level of experience to the task. That makes the process more difficult to explain to a subordinate.

The following table will help you distinguish between necessary and discretionary tasks. The tasks in the left column are more likely to be ones that you can and should delegate.

Necessary	Discretionary
To oversee the stockroom inventory count	To check on the efficiency of the stockroom operation
To check each department's overtime records	To consult with foremen on how to hold down overtime costs
To reconcile bank statements with in-house records	To evaluate new banking services
To arrange for the bonding of new employees	To discuss employees' initial performance with their supervisors
To review district sales figures	To give a pep talk to sales reps in a lagging district
To prepare a report classifying customer complaints	To discuss potential problems with a valued customer

Trivia

It's easy for managers to become involved in many tasks that have very little impact on the results they are trying to achieve. You know the type of situation. Someone has to arrange for a service contract on the photocopy machine and nobody knows whose responsibility it is; you've been asked to make a decision about the layout of the reception room; you have to preside over a meeting on the company dinner dance; a repairman shows up to work on the power lines and needs someone to explain the problem to him.

Tasks under the heading of trivia are prime targets for delegation. First, they take up your time — often a great deal of your time — without producing really important results. Second, they rarely require the skills of a manager. A subordinate can handle them adequately. Third, they are often easy to delegate. And finally, they give the delegatee a chance to exercise authority and decision making in an activity where the consequences of poor handling are not devastating.

Before you delegate a trivial task, though, ask yourself whether the job needs to be done at all. If it's little more than a time-waster, don't delegate, eliminate.

For those tasks that do need to be done, don't be offhand or careless about the delegation. Arranging a company dinner dance may not relate to the principal results you are trying to achieve, but it can affect morale. Delegate the task carefully and follow up.

Avoid the attitude, 'It's not worth delegating'. That kind of attitude is akin to the one that was expressed in the famous but pat phrase of President Jimmy Carter's Director of Office of Management and Budget, Bert Lance, when he said, 'If it ain't broke, don't fix it.' Sometimes it takes as much time to delegate as to do the task yourself. But when you take on trivial tasks yourself you get into the trivia habit. Delegating them to subordinates helps you to form the delegation habit. Look at these low-impact delegations as practice for both yourself and your subordinates. They accustom you to giving authority to your people. They teach subordinates initiative.

Specialities

The delegation of tasks that need special skills is one of the easier and more natural forms of delegation. Except for the inveterate do-it-yourselfer, few people fail to call a plumber when a pipe bursts or to ask the company lawyer to sort out a work-related legal problem.

Say you've been given the task of installing a new computerised inventory tracking system. You're a production manager, but you're familiar with the basics of data processing. You come to a point, however, where you have to choose from among various types of software for specific applications. You could research the options and make the decision yourself. Or you could delegate the task to the computer programmer who handles your department's current data processing needs.

This is a clear case for delegation. Let the subordinate apply his special knowledge to the task. Brief him on the criteria you require. Exercise control by making him report back to you before buying.

Some managers are do-it-yourselfers. They feel that every task they tackle broadens their experience and skills. But you have limited time and substantial primary duties. Suffering through the mistakes and frustrations that anyone encounters when tackling a new task is not the best way to learn. If you want to gain experience in accounting, take a seminar on the subject rather than spending long hours trying to straighten out a bookkeeping problem that your company's credit controller could solve in 20 minutes.

Delegation of specialities doesn't always involve formal skills. Many of your subordinates possess informal skills that you can draw on when delegating. For example, maybe you have a mathematical whiz as a clerk, who could check the figures in a complicated list of specifications. Perhaps you have an assistant who has demonstrated the ability to spot quickly developing trends in your industry. You might send that person to a trade convention rather than attending yourself.

Chores

Chores may fall under other categories, such as routine, necessity, and trivia. But the one characteristic that always marks a chore is that you don't like doing it.

Anything can become a chore. Consider those long drawn-out meetings that sap time and produce few results; reports you've completed many times before; complex scheduling; tedious research. With too much repetition, all these tasks can become dull and dreaded. And the best way to rid yourself of them is to delegate.

For example, the office manager of a printing company drew up a schedule of the department's work each month. The job was tedious and complicated. The manager hated it. He decided to delegate the task to a subordinate. While it took considerable time to break in the subordinate, the delegation freed the manager from a chore without impairing the results achieved. He devised a sturdy system of controls to make sure the scheduling went smoothly. For the subordinate, the broader responsibilities meant an expanded view of her department's functioning, a new challenge, an escape from the monotony of her chores.

Some managers shy away from delegating chores. They feel uneasy about pushing on to subordinates jobs that they don't care to do themselves. But again, time is the crucial factor. If you had unlimited time, you could afford to pitch in and help with the dirty work. You don't. You should focus on the tasks that need your attention and delegate anything that you can delegate.

Two other factors justify delegation of chores. First, as noted, a chore to you may be a reward to a subordinate. Take travel, for instance. What are routine trips to you may be chances for subordinates to broaden their perspectives and break out of the tedium of their normal duties. The preparation of reports may bore you, but they could fascinate subordinates. Any delegation, properly accomplished, implies trust and confers responsibility. These qualities often make up for the fact that the job is time-consuming or tedious.

Second, because delegated tasks are new to your subordinates, they may bring to these tasks interests and enthusiasm that allow them to do the tasks better than you would have done. Delegation removes routine tasks that may cause you to procrastinate or that you approach only half-heartedly.

Pet projects

It may seem paradoxical to delegate the aspects of your job that you most enjoy. Yet these are often the tasks that you hang on to even though they don't represent the best use of your time and energy. They may be related to your area of expertise or to earlier positions you've had with the company. Andrew C Sigler, chairman and chief executive officer of Champion International Corporation, a forest products company, characterises this syndrome as turf mentality. Holding on to jobs or duties becomes managers' means of protecting their turfs. Some managers cannot seem to let go of their pet projects.

For example, the head of computer operations at a chemical company enjoyed getting involved in the intricacies of programming. A former programmer, she could often quickly devise innovative solutions to data processing problems. She got into the habit of tackling many difficult programming assignments. The time she devoted to solving them drained away her attention from her genuine managerial duties.

The solution — delegate. The manager shouldn't have written programs just because she liked to. She should have delegated all programming to her subordinates and, to paraphrase Shakespeare, clasped to her soul the real jobs of managing 'with hoops of steel'.

Naturally, this doesn't mean that you need to delegate

every pleasant aspect of your job. Many true managerial tasks are enjoyable. The point made here is that you risk retaining easily delegable tasks simply because they're your pet projects.

Tasks not to delegate

The slogan 'Delegate Everything' has to be followed by the warning: 'Except . . .'

Certain tasks you should seldom delegate. Many managers err on the side of retaining too many tasks to do themselves. A few go too far in the opposite direction. Delegation doesn't work, or is inappropriate, in some areas. Delegating these types of tasks can catapult you into hot water.

Tasks that generally should not be delegated fall under the following headings:

- Ritual
- Policy making
- Specific personnel matters
- Crises
- Confidential matters

Ritual

Some duties depend more on your position than on your skills. While anyone could do them, only you can do them effectively because of who or what you are. Such tasks call for your position, your prestige, your title.

For example, a US research engineer located at a research and development lab in a city away from company headquarters was retiring after 30 years on the job. The trip to attend his retirement dinner would take the company|president half a day. He considered sending a subordinate, his vice president of administration. But in thinking over the matter, he realised that the award he was to present to the engineer would have less significance coming from anyone but the president. Not only the retiring researcher, but also his colleagues, would feel the slight. In the light of the engineer's many contributions to the company over the years, the president felt that the man deserved the honour. This was a task that he shouldn't — and didn't — delegate.

Policy making

Policy sets the limits of decision making. Managers can delegate tasks to be accomplished within established policies. They should not delegate responsibilities that require the delegatees to make decisions that actually determine policy.

The case of a personnel manager at a computer company illustrates this principle. Several assistants helped her screen job applicants. She delegated all screening to them, though she retained ultimate responsibility for hiring. As a control, she had set up strict guidelines concerning the criteria for rejecting an applicant. This was a proper delegation.

If, however, this manager had told her assistants to create their own criteria for accepting or rejecting a candidate, she would have delegated improperly. Her assistants would then be making policy, not following it. If any of them had made decisions based on racial or sexual discrimination, the manager and ultimately the company would have been liable.

Policies need not be formal. For example, companies may not have specific trade credit policies. Decisions on granting or not granting credit to potential customers may be left to the judgement of their credit controllers.

Since the credit controllers can't review every application, many of them delegate to individual sales representatives the authority to grant credit within specific limits. Cases outside these limits, the reps pass on to their credit controllers. The controllers' decisions are based on the financial conditions of the potential customers and the prevailing market and business environment.

In effect, credit controllers' decisions set their companies' credit policies at any given time. For this reason, they cannot delegate to their sales reps unlimited authority to make credit decisions. In that case, all representatives would be creating their own credit policies. These decisions might not always be in their companies' best interests.

Specific personnel matters

A large part of a manager's responsibility involves working with people. Every contact you have with one of your subordinates involves a human element, a crossflow of emotions and perceptions. Because these contacts involve subtle nuances, you should rarely delegate specific personnel-related matters. A few examples will illustrate this principle:

Evaluation

The manager of the shipping department at a clothing company had been asked to recommend one of his clerks to participate in a training programme on applications of microcomputers. He felt that three subordinates qualified for the programme. He had to choose one of them.

A despatcher who also reported to the manager had worked with all three clerks. The manager may profit from asking the despatcher's opinion about the clerks' skills and attitudes, but should not delegate the actual choice to the despatcher. The manager cannot be sure that the despatcher is unbiased and objective. The choice is his and cannot be delegated.

Discipline

Firing or reprimanding a subordinate for a misdeed or error is often an unpleasant task. A manager may be tempted to delegate it to someone else. This is always an improper use of delegation. Disciplinary matters, particularly those that result in termination of employment, are managerial duties, pure and simple. A manager has both practical and moral responsibility to handle these matters directly.

The practical aspect of a manager's responsibility to handle personally, rather than delegate, the discharge of an employee has become highlighted by the increasing number of tribunal appeals based on claims of wrongful dismissal.

Praise

Concerning a direct subordinate, a manager says to his assistant, 'Tell Mary I think she's doing a great job. I appreciate her efforts on this project.' The assistant conveys the message, but Mary is not impressed. Second-hand praise carries far less force than direct expressions of appreciation or gratitude. In fact, Mary may resent the fact that after the extra effort she put in on the project, her boss didn't even take the time personally to offer her a kind word.

Resolution of disputes

You are a supervisor and two of your foremen are involved in a controversy over priorities on the use of a machine. You cannot assign the resolution of the question to an assistant or another foreman and expect good results. As the

53

direct supervisor of the two people involved, you should handle the matter yourself. The complexity and volatility of interpersonal relationships makes this an inappropriate area to delegate.

Delegation itself

Don't delegate delegation. That is, when you pass on a task to a subordinate that involves authority and decision making, convey the facts about the job to that person directly. Don't rely on a third party.

For example, the manager of an insurance company's branch office asked a management trainee to evaluate potential vendors of office machine service. The subordinate rendered a report discussing five different companies. The manager liked the report and decided to delegate to the trainee the task of choosing a vendor and negotiating the agreement.

Fine. However, the manager suddenly had to fly to an important meeting at company headquarters that kept him away from the office for three days. He authorised his assistant to give the subordinate the green light to choose a vendor. But, he said, the trainee should report back to him, not to the assistant, if the cost exceeded the budget estimate. The assistant passed on the message, but was unclear about the exact conditions of the delegation. The trainee proceeded in good faith, but ran into problems because, after negotiating a contract, he found that he had exceeded the limits set in the budget.

Though the manager acted correctly in delegating this task, he should have called in the trainee and delegated directly, not passed the delegation itself to another person. Delegation as an interpersonal task requires a manager's direct attention.

Handling crises

A good manager avoids crises through adequate planning. Emergencies, however, inevitably arise from time to time. In most cases, you should handle crises personally rather than delegate them to subordinates.

Because a crisis by definition involves unique elements, you can't impose fully workable controls on the delegatee. You can establish guidelines for all of the unforeseen circumstances that call for decisions.

For example, the project manager for a firm of consulting engineers suddenly learned that a client company needed the firm's recommendation before it could tender for a large construction project. However, the data bank that the consultants relied on for information on this project was unavailable due to a computer malfunction. Someone had to handle the situation — had to deal with the client, evaluate alternatives, and make choices.

The manager could not delegate the handling of this type of crisis even to a very capable subordinate. Too many uncertainties were involved. In fact, the problem was solved by a decision that only the project manager himself could make. He exceeded budget and drew on another data bank. It sounds as simple as filling in a loan application, but thousands of pounds were involved for the engineering firm and millions for the client. No delegatee could have handled this crisis.

Confidential matters

Maintaining the secrecy of confidential information is a vital responsibility for a manager. Clearly, any delegation that requires you to reveal confidential information is inappropriate. Many kinds of personnel data, certain customer information, specific salaries for certain persons, trade secrets, security data, and similar matters, often fall into the confidential category.

For example, management asked its personnel manager to draw up a report classifying disciplinary actions taken in the division. The data could easily have been drawn from employee records. The manager considered delegating the task to a clerk but decided against it. Company policy regarded all disciplinary information as confidential except under certain circumstances. Although the manager trusted the clerk, he felt — correctly — that it was inappropriate to delegate a task that would give the clerk free access to disciplinary information.

Finding opportunities to delegate

The worksheet on page 56 provides you with a convenient means to evaluate the tasks you currently perform and to

55

Form to target opportunities to delegate

1. Task	2. Reason to delegate/not delegate	3. Who could handle it	4. Preparation needed	5. Quality of results	6. Delegation rating
Review and summarise production reports	Routine, necessity	Steve, Jane	Explanation; authority to collect data	Satisfactory	C
Quarterly performance appraisals	Personnel	–	–	–	A
Check on stockroom inventory	Routine, chore	George	Explanation supervised dry run	Adequate	C

spot opportunities for delegation.

List in the first column each separate task that you handle. You may also want to list some duties that you know will shortly become your own responsibility. Don't leave out minor or brief jobs that collectively take up a great deal of your time. Keep your eyes open for simple time-wasters. Consider weeding them out of your routine altogether. A few rows are filled in for each column to illustrate how you should use the form.

In the second column, identify any aspects of the task that indicate it would or would not be a good task to delegate. As previously stated, factors pointing towards delegation are: routine, necessity, trivia, speciality, chore, and pet project. Factors that indicate delegation is not appropriate include: ritual, policy making, personnel matters, crises, and confidential matters.

Next, in column 3, list for each task all of your subordinates who could possibly handle that duty. The next chapter shows you how to choose the best of these candidates.

Write down in the fourth column whatever authority, instructions, or training you would need to give so that the delegatee could perform the task satisfactorily.

Column 5 gives you a place to estimate how well the person would perform the task. You can also list any significant problems that might arise: would it take the person an inordinate amount of time? Would the results the person achieves be acceptable if not perfect?

In the last column, give the task a delegation rating from the following list. Target your delegation efforts on the tasks rated C and D.

A — I must do it myself, cannot delegate it.
B — I should do it myself, could delegate it if necessary.
C — I could do it myself, should delegate it if possible.
D — I must delegate it (eg I haven't the skills to do it).

Filling in the form will give you a running start on choosing what to delegate. But don't be content to fill in this form just once. Make it a regular habit. After all, as time passes by your own responsibilities will change; you'll have different persons reporting to you; those persons' skills and capabilities will change — for the better, you hope, but change they will.

You'll find the form a working tool that you can use for

the rest of your career. Your subordinates who also delegate will find it equally valuable, as will your peers. Share it. Shared knowledge always brings its own rewards.

Chapter 4

Selecting the Delegatee

Ralph Morris, the data processing manager for a pharmaceutical company, sat in his office one afternoon thinking about delegation. He had chosen a task that seemed well suited for passing on to one of his subordinates. Now he was wrestling with the problem of which of his people to assign the duty to.

It is that problem, choosing the right delegatee, that this chapter treats. You'll learn the importance of assessing your subordinates' capabilities; picking your own goals for delegating; considering workloads, skills, and experience; knowing your company's internal politics; and how much weight you should give to the direct results that you want to achieve.

The task that Ralph had in mind involved conducting a company-wide survey of the use of desk-top computers. His department advised managers in other areas of the company on personal computer applications, coordinated the purchase of the hardware, and helped out on problems that arose. But to keep tabs on the actual uses of the machines and to determine what effects they might have on the company's overall data processing systems, Ralph had to visit regularly each worksite where a person was using a microcomputer. During such visits he also looked for other jobs that could be computerised to make the programme more cost-effective.

Both routine and necessary, this task fitted perfectly the criteria given in the previous chapter for delegation. Ralph also felt that conducting the survey would provide the subordinate with a broader view of the firm's operations and help that person to 'look beyond the disk drives'. Because this survey played an important role in setting the company's data procrressing strategy, Ralph wanted to make sure that he picked the right person for the job.

Know your people

Ralph Morris had a head start in selecting the right delegatee: he knew thoroughly the people who worked under him. He knew that delegation is a personal process.

You cannot delegate effectively if you select the delegatee arbitrarily. And you cannot delegate effectively if you have only a superficial knowledge of your subordinates. That's like trying to play a round of golf on an unfamiliar course — you're likely to end up in hidden bunkers.

Who is the right person? What skills and experience does that person have? How broad is his or her knowledge? What about personal qualities such as working well with others, listening, regard by peers? What are his or her interests and attitudes? These are a few of the questions you should ask yourself.

Some managers discount this type of 'feel' for the people working for them. Some aren't interested. Others don't think that it's right to become too familiar with a subordinate. Still others are afraid of invading the person's privacy.

But delegation gets best results only when you assign the right task to the right person. Otherwise you will repeatedly encounter frustration and failure. And selecting the right person means knowing more about that person than where his or her desk is located.

Knowing your people doesn't mean you have to join them at the local pub or sit in on lunch-hour gossip sessions. It means you have to be observant and interested in how they do their jobs, and listen to their suggestions, ideas, and complaints. And it means you have to reach out from time to time to gain a sense of the person as a person, not just as a worker. That includes, at times, understanding their family problems, hearing of the victories and defeats in their lives outside the workplace, and giving them time to tell you about their personal aspirations in their private lives as well as on the job.

What's your goal?

Delegation has three general goals. In choosing the right

delegatee, you have to weigh these goals to decide which are the most important for this task.

1. Direct results

When you delegate to a subordinate the compilation of an inventory report, for example, the main thing you're interested in is a list of figures. For most cases of delegation, the direct result is the most important goal. But you should also keep in mind the two other important goals.

2. Development

When you delegate the task of inspecting the company's facilities and reporting on compliance with work rules, your primary interest may not be in the report itself as much as in the fact that the tour broadens the delegatee's view of the firm's operations, thereby contributing to experience and development. Development always represents an important delegation goal and complicates the selection of the delegatee. You want the right person, not necessarily the most competent person. You'll read more about this aspect of delegation later in this chapter.

3. Evaluation

It should be clear to you that your subordinates will sooner or later have to be tested under fire. In some delegations your main goal will be to see how the person performs in a given situation. But still, you don't delegate with the expectation of failure. To do so would ultimately reflect unfavourably on you. And, it would be about as useful in accomplishing your objectives as would have been the captain of the *Titanic* telling the steward to rearrange the deck chairs.

Current work load

The first name that came to Ralph Morris's mind to handle the personal computer survey was Stan Bingham. Stan served as his liaison with the financial controller's office. A capable young manager — bright, energetic, and a good communicator — Stan had the qualifications for the job. Ralph had delegated tasks to him before and Stan had completed them successfully. Moreover, Ralph had found him to be highly motivated and careful about details.

The problem, though, was that in addition to his day-to-day duties, Stan was involved in writing an integrated accounting software program. Ralph knew that Stan would accept yet another assignment and try to do a good job, but he didn't feel that he should further increase his subordinate's workload. His work on the software package really merited his undivided attention. When he finished it, he would be ready for further delegations, but now was not the time.

Whether a subordinate can handle a new task without it interfering with his current duties should always be considered when you choose a delegatee. Not only is it unfair to add to the work of an already burdened subordinate, but it invites poor performance in either the primary duties, the delegated task, or both.

Weigh this question carefully, though. A delegated task need not detract from the performance of a delegatee's primary responsibilities. The opposite can happen. Frequently, adding new tasks actually increases productivity of subordinates in their main duties. They feel that their jobs have been enriched, that they have received recognition of their abilities, even that they may soon be on the fast track to success. For example, a production supervisor assigned quality control duties may not only do a good job filing quality reports; the delegation may boost his morale and cause him to work more effectively on his regular job.

Skills required

June Baker's name was the next to come to Ralph's mind as a potential delegatee. She needed to get some experience outside her current duties as senior programmer. She was both meticulous about details and eager to learn. Her current responsibilities didn't put any special strains on her time. She could easily fit the survey into her schedule.

But Ralph decided against assigning her the task. While she knew programming inside out, she knew very little about microcomputers. This task required that the person be able to talk intelligently about current applications and be able to spot potential new ones. Such a person needed at least some familiarity with micros. Ralph decided either to find a task better suited for June to get her feet wet in this area or to encourage her to take a course in the subject.

When selecting the delegatee, ask yourself, 'Does this task require special skills or knowledge?' If so, those skills should be a primary criterion for guiding your selection. Naturally, a person should pick up new skills in the process of completing the task. But to delegate to a person who does not have the necessary basic skills to get the job done is like sending a novice boxer into the ring with a pro — he may learn something, but he may also be knocked out before he has a chance to.

Independent experience

Another subordinate Ralph considered for the task was his operations assistant, Tony Gallo. Tony had done some work with microcomputers when the company first installed them. A good worker, he could easily have fitted the extra assignment into his routine. But Ralph hesitated to give him the go-ahead.

The survey usually took the better part of a week to conduct plus another couple of days of analysis. While Ralph was satisfied with Tony's specific abilities, he knew that the subordinate had always worked under close supervision in the main computer centre. He didn't feel that he should suddenly send Tony out to work on his own for such a lengthy period of time. Later, maybe, he'd be ready. But for now, Ralph wanted to give Tony more limited assignments that would allow him to exercise his initiative and self-direction gradually. He was afraid that, given Tony's current experience, his chances of making a botch of the survey were too great.

Experience differs from skills or knowledge. Recent business administration graduates may have analytical skills and theoretical knowledge. But they need experience to teach them how to motivate others and how to exercise authority effectively before they can be assigned the task of managing an operation.

Be careful of trying to force-feed experience to

subordinates. People can learn to swim by gradually practising and perfecting the strokes. But throwing them into the deep end of the pool is a sure way to make them afraid of the water.

Personal qualities

'I could give this to Barry Ellis,' Ralph speculated, thinking of his senior systems analyst. 'He knows personal computers. He's been in the department for years, so he's certainly had enough experience. He has the time. But . . .'

It didn't take much consideration for Ralph to figure out why he didn't want to assign the survey to Barry. The man was competent, yes. He did his job satisfactorily. But he was only three years away from retirement. Furthermore, he had never shown the spark, the eagerness and motivation, that some of the other people in the department did. To him, the survey wouldn't be an opportunity to show his stuff. It would be just another chore to finish. He'd tackle the assignment all right, with all the eagerness of a child turning off the television after being told to go to bed. He wouldn't bring to the job the enthusiasm and energy that it called for.

Barry had some other personal qualities that made him unsuitable, too. He had little patience with the opinions of others. Worse, he let them know it. Plus, he preferred to talk rather than to listen. This survey called for a different type of person, one open to the thoughts and ideas of other people and willing to pay genuine attention to them.

Of all the personal qualities that you should consider when picking a delegatee, attitude is the most important. Is the person eager to move forward in power and position? Or do you have a hard time interesting him or her in anything except a weekly pay packet? Does that person approach a new task with a desire to learn? Or does he or she see every work assignment as a burden? All the other qualifications mean little if the person has the wrong attitude. Like a racing yacht rigged for speed, but with its bottom fouled with barnacles, such persons won't make much progress no matter how well you trim the sails.

An ability to work with people is often an important personal qualification for successful completion of a delegated job, duty, or task. Some of your people have charisma, a personal magic of leadership that arouses special enthusiasm having nothing to do with their positions. Others can't seem to elicit the cooperation of others no matter how many carrots they dangle before them. Some can communicate eloquently. Others with equally sound ideas have trouble getting them across. Some put the people they work with at ease; others put them on edge. All of these characteristics will have a significant impact on the successful outcome of any task you delegate that requires working with others.

Many other qualities will guide your selection. Is the person careful? Observant? Suited to long hours of detailed work? Able to handle frustration? Mature? Thoughtful? Impulsive? Decisive? Dependent? Easily flustered?

Negative qualities are as important to examine as are positive. For example, suppose your company wants to introduce a new quality awareness programme. You need someone to lead small groups of workers in discussions of the importance of product quality. Delegate this task to a person who tries to dictate to the workers rather than elicit their cooperation, and he or she will be about as successful in getting results as the proverbial salesman when selling refrigerators to Eskimos.

Power abusers − those who like to exercise authority for its own sake rather than as a tool to achieve goals − make poor candidates for most delegated tasks. Not only do they fail, they also create ill will among other employees.

Many other personal qualities should make you think twice about assigning the subordinate an important delegation. Beware of lazy, careless, argumentative, uncooperative, or vindictive people. Maybe they have short fuses or generally can't get along with others. While negative traits may not preclude all delegation, they should alert you to select with care.

Again, your goals for delegating will play a role in your decision. Are you interested only in the direct results? Then you won't delegate the task of reviewing long, complex, statistical reports to a subordinate with a short attention span. But if development is your aim, you might delegate the task of conducting a group of visitors through the plant to a subordinate who needs experience in communicating with outsiders. Or you may want a subordinate who you suspect is quick to anger to handle a particularly vexing production snag so you can evaluate performance under pressure.

Company politics

For a moment, Ralph thought he'd hit on the ideal person to go ahead with the survey. Don Foley, the data entry supervisor, had all the right qualifications. He had broad computer skills. He knew personal computers. He knew how to listen. He was amiable. He was chomping at the bit for more challenging work. And he'd proved himself to be a self-starter.

But then Ralph thought about the politics of the situation. He wouldn't be making the delegation in a vacuum. Everyone in the department would know about it. And Don had only been on the staff for three weeks. His fellow workers hadn't resented his being hired. They knew that no one inside the company had been ready to move into the position. And Don got along well with them since he'd started working.

But Ralph knew that conducting the personal computer survey was considered something of a plum. The person selected would have a leg up on a very important direction for data processing in the company. To give the job to a new employee would't go down well. Not only would others resent it, the appointment of Don Foley might backfire on both Don and Ralph. One thing the person selected would need was cooperation.

In a few months, after Don had been accepted as 'one of the group', the situation would be different. Right now, Ralph felt that politically he wouldn't be the right person to delegate to.

You can never neglect company politics when delegating. Social factors play an important role in the functioning of any organisation. If you always hand Roy the choice assignments and give Mary the dirty work, then not only is Mary going to resent you, but the rest of your subordinates are likely to turn on you as well — and maybe on Roy, too.

Sometimes you may be tempted to delegate repeatedly to a particular person, especially if you have one very competent subordinate. But you'll find it better to resist the urge and to play fairly. Developing teamwork is an important part of a manager's job. Thoughtless or lopsided delegation can undermine teamwork in ways that are hard to repair.

Making the right choice

Though Ralph considered and eliminated several subordinates before making his final selection, he'd kept in the back of his mind one person whom he might pick. Marsha Reed, his operations coordinator, had plenty of work of her own to do, but she wasn't too burdened to fit the periodic survey into her routine. She'd occasionally used microcomputers and had a keen interest in them and their applications. In the past she'd handled a number of tasks that showed her ability to work on her own, meet deadlines, and overcome unexpected difficulties.

Moreover, Marsha wanted to learn new skills and broaden her involvement in the company's data processing function. She was observant and got along well with others. Her main weakness was difficulty expressing her ideas in writing. Ralph thought this assignment would give her good experience because she would need to summarise her findings in a written report. As a result, Ralph selected her to conduct the survey, confident that he had made the right choice.

It's important when selecting the right delegatee to organise objectively your opinions about each possible candidate. On page 68 is a tool for turning vague notions about the task and the candidate into specific ideas. Using it will help you to weigh the pros and cons of each candidate and to match the right person with the right task.

The worksheet gives an example of how this tool might have been used by Ralph Morris. Draw up your own chart to use for your delegation decisions. Other people in your company who delegate will also find this form an excellent guide and helpful aid to decision making.

Special delegations

Some special tasks will lead you to select either an expert or a personal assistant as the delegatee. These assignments require a slightly different approach:

Delegatee evaluation worksheet

Task: To conduct quarterly survey of current and potential uses of microcomputers throughout the company and to write a report on findings and recommendations

Principal goal: Direct results   Time required: Approx. 1½ weeks   Deadline: 23/4

Qualifications	Work load	Skills	Experience	Personal	Other
Necessary	Can devote 1½ weeks each quarter	Knows micro applications, edp basics	Has worked with deadlines; self-direction	Listener; observant; innovative	
Preferred	—	Some knowledge of non-computer operations	Interpersonal; work outside edp department	Communicator; logical	
Candidates					
Stan	No, too busy	Good	OK	OK	
June	OK	Needs more background in micros	OK	Good	
Tony	OK	OK	No, needs seasoning	Good	
Barry	OK	Good	Good	No, too abrasive; lacks enthusiasm	
Don	OK	Good	Yes, with former employer	OK	Needs a chance to fit in; too new
Marsha	OK	Good	OK	OK, but needs to take care writing report	

Note: edp = electronic data processing

Delegating to an assistant

When you delegate to a personal secretary, an administrative assistant, or anyone else who works closely with you, you should pay attention to the following points:

- *Don't take the delegation for granted.* Use the same care and results-oriented approach that you would with any other subordinate.
- *Make it clear that you are giving over decision-making authority.* Otherwise, the assistant may think it necessary to check with you as a matter of course.
- *Delegate to develop.* Your personal assistant deserves as much chance to develop new skills and experience as any other subordinate. And you will profit as the person becomes increasingly competent.
- *Don't forget to give credit.* If an assistant has played an important role in a task, make sure he or she gets all due credit. Your hogging the glory will jeopardise the success of future delegations.

Delegating to an expert

This includes delegation to a lawyer, an accountant, a computer programmer, or even a management consultant. Remember the following:

- *Be sure of qualifications.* Don't assume that every lawyer knows patent law, or that every accountant is a tax expert. Size up the expert, as you would any other delegatee, according to skills, experience, and personal qualifications.
- *Retain responsibility.* Since you are ultimately responsible for a delegated task, be sure to monitor the expert's work. Try to pick up enough basic knowledge of the expert's area of special know-how to get a sense of whether the expert is on the right track. Get a second opinion on vital matters.
- *Set criteria.* Remember that you have to play a role in setting up the objectives of the assignment. A lawyer may be able to advise you on some of the points to include in a legal document, but you will have to convey to the lawyer the ultimate goal of drawing up the document. In the same way, you will have to be

clear in explaining to a programmer what you want a particular software program to accomplish.

Delegate to develop

As pointed out earlier in this chapter, you must weigh your own goals when selecting the right person to delegate to. Getting the result you want is important, of course. But you may often find opportunities to delegate tasks where the goal of developing the delegatee's skills is paramount, and the direct result of lesser consequence.

Give some thought to this analogy. Learning to fly an aeroplane consists of three stages. First, students learn the principles of aerodynamics from books and on-the-ground instruction. Next, they handle the controls of the plane in flight under the watchful eyes of instructors. Finally, they go up for solo flights. Just as no one can be considered a competent pilot who hasn't soloed, neither would any instructor send up a student alone before the person was ready. Instructors give novices many opportunities to develop gradually both their skills and confidence.

Delegation involves a similar process. You try to guide the subordinate toward competence and independence. You don't send the person out on a solo flight right off the bat, thereby encouraging a crash into serious problems. Neither do you deny the person the opportunity to 'take the stick', to learn by doing.

The ability to develop good subordinates is a key skill that separates truly superlative managers from merely competent ones. This skill gives you three big pluses: first your current organisation runs at top efficiency. Second, having skilful, experienced people under you hastens your own promotion. And third, developing subordinates who are promoted into other areas of your company builds for you a network of grateful and trusted allies.

Your people will develop in many ways. Just learning the ropes and observing how things are done will make them more experienced. So will formal training courses, lectures, and seminars. But a rule of thumb holds that 90 per cent of a manager's ability is developed through experience. Experience means delegation.

Delegation to develop forces you to look at the long term, not just the immediate results desired. Don't always pick the most competent subordinate for the task at hand. Don't always look over the shoulder of the person you delegate to. Give that person enough leeway to learn even if the direct results are not the best possible ones.

Selecting the task for development

An accounting supervisor at a large food processing company had on his staff a bright young tax specialist. This woman handled her primary duties with great care and had suggested a number of innovative solutions to problems. The supervisor's opinion of her, though, was not shared by all of his peers. The woman had made presentations at a number of interdepartmental meetings. She always seemed unprepared, even inept. When she couldn't answer questions quickly and briefly, she became flustered and confused.

The supervisor knew that the woman's weakness was not in her accounting knowledge and skills, but rather in her aversion to speaking in public. The task that he decided to delegate to her, then, was not a complex tax problem that she could work on by herself. Instead, he had her run an orientation programme for a group of sandwich students who would be working in the department. He told her to give the various groups an introductory lecture, show them around the department, and answer their questions.

This supervisor was delegating to the woman's weakness. She was not the best subordinate to handle the task. Rather, the task was a good one for her because it allowed her to develop her self-confidence. It gave her an opportunity to practise speaking and thinking on her feet, yet the direct result if she failed would not be disastrous. He didn't risk a major failure by, for example, asking her to chair all by herself an interdepartmental meeting. This was a clear case of delegating to develop.

Of course, you won't want to delegate every task to overcome weaknesses. In fact, delegation to build on strengths is also a part of development. The supervisor might next ask this subordinate to devise a major new tax strategy. This would also encourage her development by broadening her view of the company and further practising her analytical and decision-making abilities.

Almost everyone can profit from some form of delegation. The perennially careless employee may be just the person to pass out a new pamphlet on safety and discuss it with fellow workers. The quality control supervisor who doesn't like to write may be the person to assign to drawing up a draft of a report on production efficiency. It is a mark of a keen manager to be able to match challenging tasks with the proper subordinates.

A series of successes

When Sugar Ray Leonard — considered one of the most skilled boxers in history — began his professional career, his handlers didn't immediately schedule a bout with the champion. Instead, they set up a series of warm-up fights against progressively tougher opponents. This allowed Leonard gradually to hone his talent without having his confidence undermined by a premature loss. This series of successes prepared him to win the world championship.

In the same way, when Henry Ford II retired as head of the Ford Motor Co. in 1979, he made it clear that he hoped his only son Edsel would some day follow in his footsteps. He did not, however, encourage the Ford directors to immediately put the 30-year-old Edsel at the helm of the giant company, where the consequences of failure would be catastrophic. Rather, the heir apparent would have to work his way through a long executive management programme. When his father stepped down, Edsel was serving as the assistant managing director of Ford's Australian subsidiary. Again, here is an example of a series of successes being used to develop.

Limited delegations

Limited delegation is a good starting point for development. You might say, 'Steve, why don't you take over reviewing these production reports for a week?' Now you have a chance to see how Steve handles the job. He's on his own, but you're right behind him, just like the flight instructor, ready to take over if he gets into trouble. If, at the end of the week, Steve has proved himself, you can extend the delegation, perhaps put it on a permanent basis. If the job has been too much for him, the limited delegation gives you a graceful way to take back the job.

Or you might say, 'Betty, could you write up the tender specs on this project for me? I'll need them in two weeks.' Then, if Betty does a good job on the specs, maybe you will go ahead and let her handle the entire tendering and vendor selection process. You've given her a limited delegation.

Be sure in making limited delegations that you truly do delegate. If the trainer always has his hand on the controls, the novice pilot doesn't really get a feel for flying. Make sure you put at least some of the decision making in the hands of the subordinate. Give the person room to manoeuvre.

Learning from mistakes

Helping a delegatee grow and improve through devising a series of successes does not mean that you are seeking to avoid all mistakes when you delegate. In fact, mistakes are an essential part of learning through experience. Mistakes aptly illustrate what not to do. And the person who has learned what not to do is wiser than the person who has never been allowed to venture far enough to make an error.

Of course you don't want your subordinates to make so many errors that they are intimidated by them. So you limit the chances for mistakes. For example, a shipping manager asks his assistant to work out a schedule for the next month. The assistant knows that overtime costs are a concern of the company, so he devises a tight schedule of shipments that limits labour costs. While the manager delegates the scheduling, he retains responsibility for approving the schedule before it is implemented. After looking over the subordinate's work, he calls him in and points out that the schedule doesn't leave enough time for changing over some of the packing machinery or for contingencies.

Here, the subordinate made a mistake. The shipping manager's control, though, limited the damage. Perhaps after the assistant draws up the schedule a few more times, his boss will let him set it in motion immediately. If no controls had been included with the original assignment the mistake could have been costly. Shipments would have been delayed. More importantly, the mistake might have bruised the assistant's confidence, making him over-cautious and wary of making decisions.

Your third goal in selection

Evaluation

You can learn a great deal about potential delegatees by letting them participate. Participation should begin with setting objectives. Say you're an inventory manager. You want your assistant to draw up a report on ways to trim inventory. Begin by asking for ideas on the report's structure, broken down by building, by product line, or by some other classification. When possible, let the delegatee select the structure. That task encourages participation.

Always emphasise results. Why are we doing this report? What are our goals? Can we quantify them? For example, can we target a 5 per cent reduction as an objective? Again, let the delegatee offer input.

When you delegate to a person for the first time, you should take care to explain the meaning of delegation. Let delegates know that, within certain prescribed limits, they're on their own. Let them know that, in addition to leaving yourself more time for other duties and getting the task done, you are delegating to help them get a broader view of the company, to get used to shouldering responsibility, or for the purpose of evaluating their abilities.

On your side, listening is an important part of delegation for evaluation. For example, maybe a subordinate lets on that this assignment is beyond his or her capabilities. The subordinate may not come out and say so, but careful listening can alert you. Perhaps you can overcome the problem through encouragement, or by delegating a less extensive, confidence-boosting assignment.

Guidance

Controls are important in all forms of delegation. They are

especially important with delegations aimed at evaluation because they provide a safety net for a potentially valuable subordinate.

Coaching, advice, and minor correction to keep the delegatee on course are the most important types of control for the person who is learning a new skill. Casually asking, 'How's it going?' gives subordinates a chance to bring up issues that may be blocking their progress. (Controls of delegated jobs, duties and tasks will be covered in detail in later chapters.)

For example, you've delegated to an assistant the task of monitoring and reporting on scrap levels in your department. You observe that she is spending a great deal of time keeping track of bulky sheet steel scrap and less time on faulty electronic components. Without actually telling her how to handle the task, you might point out to her the importance of value differentials in scrap control and the much higher value represented by the electronic components. You have not only controlled the delegation, but you have also added to your evaluation of this subordinate as a proper choice for this or future tasks to be delegated.

Feedback

When the novice pilot first takes control of the plane, he or she experiences new sensations, and is not sure if this is the way flying should feel. Gradually, with experience and feedback from the instructor, the student develops a feel for handling the aircraft.

Feedback is also important in delegation. A word of encouragement from you not only tells delegatees that they've made the right decision, but also lets them know that they were right to make a decision. It encourages independence.

A formal evaluation session after a delegated task is completed can also help you when your goal in choosing a delegatee is evaluation. It gives the subordinate a chance to review decisions made with you. It lets you give encouragement as well as suggest how the delegatee could have made the job easier. It allows both of you a chance to review the delegatee's progress and talk about other delegations that may aid his or her development. And, it gives you one more piece to solve the puzzle of selecting the right persons for delegated tasks.

Chapter 5

The Techniques of Effective Delegation

'I know why to delegate and what I want to delegate. I've chosen the right person. Now how do I go about actually passing on the assignment?' The answer: you prepare in advance, you come to a clear agreement with your subordinate on results, timing, and resources. And you follow through.

This chapter discusses the techniques of delegation. Important as these basic principles are, though, keep in mind that they are only the beginning. Technique does not turn a painter into a Picasso. The rules that follow are only the foundation of the art of delegation.

A tale of two managers

Barry Stanton and Hal Baker were both department supervisors at a large financial services company. Both performed their duties competently. But each felt the need to delegate more work to his subordinates, not only to ease his own workload, but also to give his people wider experience. Each sat down and selected a number of appropriate tasks for delegation and carefully chose the subordinates best suited for the purpose. The results that each attained, though, were not the same.

Barry had some nervous and uncertain moments in giving over decision-making authority to his people. But, generally, they came through for him. They accepted the delegations and made sincere efforts to attack the difficulties they encountered and to learn from their new tasks, duties, or jobs.

Hal ran into problems. To begin with, he thought it took so long to explain all the facts about the delegated task that delegation hardly saved him any time at all. Then, many of his subordinates kept pestering him with questions. Some to whom he delegated tasks approached the new work too casually, merely doing a superficial job. A few subordinates didn't come to Hal with problems. That made him worry so much about how they were doing that he spent a great deal of time checking up on them.

Be prepared

The difference between Hal's and Barry's experiences with delegation can be summed up in one word: preparation. Delegation works best when your style of management has prepared both you and your people to accept and benefit from the delegation process.

What is a 'delegation style' of management? It begins with team spirit. Delegation cannot work without motivation. 'I' and 'you' have to become 'we'. Your subordinates have to feel that they're part of a group effort, not just workhorses being loaded with more burdens. And they have to feel that they have the whole team behind them, that they're not being asked to crawl out on a limb alone.

An effective delegation style is always results-oriented. Some of Hal Baker's people, accustomed to just doing what they were told without regard to accomplishments, couldn't quickly fathom the importance of results. To them, *how* they did something was more important than results achieved. That attitude kills delegation. But it is an attitude that may be generated by an ineffective delegator.

Delegation flourishes in an atmosphere that emphasises rewards over punishment. Delegation requires initiative. Initiative means taking chances. Your subordinates won't take many chances if they have little to gain and a great deal to lose. Investors wouldn't put their money into growth firms if the stock offered only minimal chances for breaking even and substantial risks for bankruptcy.

Information, please

Barry and Hal differed most in their management styles when it came to their attitude towards information. Hal believed in giving his subordinates only the facts they needed to do their jobs. Not that Hal was particularly secretive. He just thought that his approach made life easier. He also felt that being 'in the know' was one of a manager's prerogatives. And the fact that Hal was not a skilful communicator reinforced the tendency.

Barry, on the other hand, felt that the more information his people had, the better. He made a point of keeping them informed not only of what was going on in relation to their individual jobs, but also of broader company goals and strategies. He filled them in on issues relating to his own job. He passed on to his key subordinates most of his informational mail and memos. Frequently, he took a subordinate along to meetings that he had with his own boss.

This open attitude towards information flow facilitated Barry's delegation efforts in two ways. First, it reinforced the team atmosphere that he emphasised. His people had a better picture of the broader objectives that they were working towards, and they knew how their individual efforts fitted it. Second, it saved Barry a great deal of time when making a delegation. For example, when he asked a subordinate to track the effects of a marketing campaign on sales, he didn't have to take time to explain the nature and purpose of the marketing effort. He'd already passed that information on in the normal course of business.

'It's not worth delegating.' 'It takes too much time to explain.' 'My people aren't ready.' All of these excuses boil down to a single fact: you're hoarding information. As a result, every delegation requires you to convey a lot of facts that the subordinate should have known already.

The value of 'soft' data

Reports, statistics, memos, and meetings can all convey factual or hard information. But when it comes to delegating, soft information plays a big role as well. You can't quantify soft information, and maybe you can't even verify it. It consists of rumours, gossip, grapevine reports, and opinions.

- A sales rep has heard that a competitor may be considering a price change.

- The production manager in Plant C is hard to get along with.
- Several companies have had maintenance problems with a machine we're thinking of purchasing.

All these are examples of soft information. They're important facts, but you won't find them in any official report.

The value of soft information — for both you and your delegatee — is that it's current. Today's rumour may become tomorrow's fact. And like a bird in the hand, a current piece of data is worth two of yesterday's facts. Tomorrow your competitor will have already put his new price into effect; you will have run up against the production manager's irascible nature in person; and the maintenance problems on the machine will be your problems.

Soft information, though, is difficult to convey effectively. It doesn't lend itself to being passed on in formal reports or memos. The best way to keep subordinates filled in is to develop open lines of communication. Encourage casual discussions with your people. You might want to schedule weekly informal 'information sessions' in which you and your people share pertinent facts, hard and soft.

Prepare yourself

Another factor that compounded Hal Baker's delegation problems was that he wasn't ready to delegate. He didn't want to give up real authority or decision making. He feared the conseque. .es of his subordinates' mistakes. This made him interfere with those few subordinates who did show some initiative.

The next chapter discusses some of the common personal obstacles that managers must overcome when they start to delegate. Bear in mind, however, that delegating is a difficult and risky procedure. When you know that you, yourself, are ready to delegate, you've taken an important preparatory step.

For this reason, you shouldn't plunge into delegation head first. Establishing an effective pattern and style of delegating takes, not weeks or months, but a year or more. And you'll never become perfect — there are always more ways to improve. Proceed surely but gradually. Don't trip over obstacles on your first attempts, then give up delegating as a lost cause.

Getting started

Many managers have trouble getting off square one when it comes to delegation. They can identify a couple of tasks they might be able to pass on to subordinates. They recognise that certain of their people would profit from taking on new duties. But they never feel the time is ripe to begin. They procrastinate, put off delegating as something to start next week.

The best way to get over this 'cold feet' syndrome is to schedule a series of idea sessions with your key subordinates. The question you should put to each one is, 'What do you feel you can contribute to this department that you aren't contributing today?' Their answers should clue you in to each person's areas of interest and enthusiasm. If, for example, a subordinate says, 'I think I could cut down on scrap', that person might be an ideal candidate to assign to do that monthly scrap report that you now handle yourself. The idea is not to let your subordinates dictate to you, but to give you ideas for moving off dead centre. Incidentally, the 'idea session' is an effective delegation technique itself.

Another good opportunity to start delegating is when a subordinate brings you an idea or suggestion. For example, one of your people says, 'I think we could cut down on data entry if we were to link these two accounting functions together and let the computer handle it.' Don't answer, 'I'll look into that, it just might be feasible.' Instead, delegate. Tell the subordinate: 'Sit down with our software people and go over it. Bring me a written report on the matter in two weeks.' Suggestions from your people give you new opportunities to delegate long after you've started.

If you're still having trouble entering the delegation 'mode', try a little job enrichment right in your own area of responsibility, as did managers of the Linde Division of Union Carbide. Management was dissatisfied with the rejection rate of torches. And the workers felt that they had little responsibility for the finished product because the process of making torches was so highly fragmented.

After study, the company changed the assembly of torches from a process involving 19 steps, six work stations, and seven pairs of hands, to a job design where each worker would do all the assembly, test the torch, and even make minor repairs. As a result, workers have a greater variety of tasks requiring more varied skills. They see the final product and can claim it as one they made themselves. And, because they do testing, they get immediate feedback on the quality of their work. Job satisfaction and productivity soared.

Job enrichment suggests many opportunities for delegating. For example, if you're an advertising account manager, maybe you can turn over some of your client contact duties to a media buyer or even a senior copywriter who wants to move into management. If you're a store manager, maybe you can delegate to your buyers some of the merchandising decisions you currently make yourself. As a production supervisor, perhaps you can allow foremen to make some quality control decisions in their own sectors.

Before you delegate

One of the tasks that gave Hal Baker problems during his initial attempt at delegating was a quarterly report on overtime expenses in his department. The report required the compilation of statistics, an analysis of trends, and suggestions for keeping costs down in the future. When Glen Elliott, one of the supervisors working under him, brought Hal some of the raw data for the report, Hal said, 'Glen, why don't you handle the whole report? You seem to know what you're doing.' Hal gave him a few tips on how he made up the report, a pat on the back, and let him proceed.

'First,' Hal later complained, 'Glen kept coming back to ask me about every little point to be covered by the report. Then, what he ended up giving me wasn't what I wanted anyway. I should have done it myself.'

Hal could have taken a lesson from Barry Stanton's handling of the same delegation for his department. He also passed on the task to a subordinate. But before doing so, he thought out and developed the results that he wanted the subordinate to achieve. He noted carefully the authority and resources that person would need. He estimated the amount of time the project would take, including a margin to compensate for the fact that the duty would be new to the person. He anticipated the questions that would be raised and even problems that the delegatee would encounter and worked out answers to them. In other words, he prepared himself. When the time came to hand over the task to the subordinate he'd chosen, the process went smoothly.

Making the delegation

The following scenario covers Barry Stanton's delegation of the overtime report to his subordinate Laura Thompson. It illustrates some of the important points to keep in mind when actually delegating to one of your people.

To begin with, note that Barry doesn't make the delegation 'on the run'. A hallway or noisy meeting is not the place to pass along the information required by an important delegation. Barry called Laura into his office when he had plenty of time and expected few interruptions.

Barry: Laura, the reason I asked you to step into my office is that it's nearly time for the quarterly overtime report and I wanted to talk with you about it. I think you've seen reports that I've done in the past, so you understand the gist of it. The corporation uses the data in cost projections and budgeting. We also take a look at them once in a while here in the department. I've decided to give you the responsibility for the report this quarter. Can you fit it into your schedule without too much trouble?

Laura: Sure. I'm working on these cost projections, you know, but I've made good progress on them already.

Barry: Right. You should be able to handle them both without one messing up the other.

Laura: I'm sure I can.

Barry: Having you handle this will help to free some of my time. And you'll learn a little more about what's going on in the department outside your own group. Now, you've had experience assigning overtime to your own people. What do you think a report like this should hit on?

83

Laura: A couple of things. First, I think the group managers should be given quite a bit of freedom in explaining what's behind the overtime. Maybe we could even add more categories for reasons, or let them explain individual situations more thoroughly. I also think the report should be written up in a format that is easier to understand. Sometimes all those statistics make tough reading.

Barry: I think you've hit on something there. The main idea here is to cut down overtime costs.

Laura: To produce a working tool for the manager.

Barry: Right. If you can do that without leaving out any information that head office require for their records, fine. But we agree on the essential point: the more the report helps keep costs down, the better.

Laura: Certainly, I understand.

Barry: Now, today's the third. The deadline for this is the thirtieth. I'd like to have a few days to look over your report myself before we send it along. How about having it on my desk by the twenty-fourth? Any problem?

Laura: Three weeks should be plenty of time.

Barry: You should probably try to get most of your data together in the first week so that you have plenty of time to let it cook. Of course, that's up to you. Why don't you give me a quick update on the fourteenth, just so I know you're moving along on it. All right?

Laura: Fine, no problem.

Barry: Oh, by the way, you may have to light a fire under some of the group managers to get them to pull the stats together. Especially the people in marketing. I'll try to smooth the way by passing the word along that you're running the show in this area. They're to give you any data you ask for and let you go over the original records if you need to. Is there anything else you might need to get the job done?

Laura: I might need some extra help from the word-processing pool to pull the final draft together.

Barry: I'll give 'em the word so they'll expect the extra work and get it out on time.

Laura: That should do it.

Barry: You can probably guess that some people don't see this as their number one priority.

Laura: What do I do if they keep putting me off?

Barry: I've always used a little bit of arm twisting and a lot of persuasion. Keep the pressure on them in a nice way, that's the main thing. And don't let it bug you.

Laura: Okay.

Barry: So we understand what we're after here. You know the timetable. I just want to emphasise that this is your bailiwick now. I'll make sure the people at head office know that these new sharp ideas coming up to them are from you. But remember, they get very peevish when they get late or incomplete data. With your experience and skills, I think you'll find this is a piece of cake. Anything big comes up — let's say a week goes by and you're still short of a large chunk of data — let me know. Otherwise, you're on your own.

Laura: I understand, Barry. I'll do my best.

The elements of effective delegation

This scenario serves only as a guide to the proper way to convey a delegated task to a subordinate. Some situations will require far more extensive explanation and discussion, others considerably less. Barry's approach does point out the most important elements of any delegation and some techniques you can use.

Results

Note that Barry does not begin by explaining in detail the steps that Laura must complete to successfully produce an overtime report. Instead, he talks first about the desired results. And, he encourages Laura to add her own thoughts. She isn't locked into a method. Rather, she agrees with her boss on an objective: to produce a tool to help cut overtime costs. She also has some suggestions for making the report more effective. You'll find many subordinates able to give you fresh ideas for improving methods, which they see from a different perspective.

Results are the key to every delegation. Make sure the objective agreed on is clear and specific. Don't allow the delegatee to lose sight of it.

Time

You and your subordinate should reach an agreement on the specific time when the task should be completed. If the delegatee has a problem with your suggested deadline, be flexible when possible and immediately work out a more suitable time limit.

Many otherwise proper delegations are ruined by uncertain or indefinite deadlines. 'As soon as possible', 'whenever you can get to it', and 'by some time next month', are all formulas for confusion and inaction. Make sure the subordinate knows that the deadline is firm.

Resources: don't half-delegate

When you half-delegate, you pass along a job but don't provide the resources to get it done. Resources can range from a simple phone call to a colleague requesting co-operation with the delegatee to multimillion pound spending authority. When you've decided what the person needs, make it clear exactly what resources are at his or her disposal. Discuss the matter with the delegatee and agree what is sufficient.

Authority is always a resource required for delegation. If you have been performing the task yourself, your position has given you the needed authority. Your subordinates do not normally have that advantage. Make sure that all persons affected by the delegation know that you've delegated authority to the person you've given the job to. In some instances, a subordinate may require some special form of authorisation. Banks require formal written authority for persons to sign cheques; or it may be less formal, such as Laura's verbally given authority to solicit data from other group managers.

Don't delegate half a task

Note that Barry doesn't have Laura collect and analyse the overtime data, then retain the recommendation section for himself. If she has the ability to undertake the first two steps, then she should be able to handle the decision-making aspect of the project, too. Always try to delegate an entire task. This heightens your subordinate's interest and sense of accomplishment. It is another technique to make your delegating effective.

Even worse than retaining part of a task to do yourself is to delegate a task to two different people. If Laura is to gather data and analyse it, and Harvey to shape the analysis into recommendations, then conflicts and confusion are almost inevitable. You must clearly define responsibilities in order to be an effective delegator.

Reasons

Tom Sawyer tricked his friends into helping him whitewash the fence by acting as if this tedious task was actually a fascinating one requiring special skill. Some managers try the same strategy when making delegations. They rarely have Tom's good luck.

If you make a delegation primarily to free your own time, be up-front with the subordinate about the reason. When you honestly feel that tackling a new task will be interesting or broadening for your delegatee, let him or her know that, too. But don't try to pass off a tedious chore as an 'exciting learning experience' when it's not. Delegation involves trust. Don't do anything with your subordinates to lose it. Sugar-coating an assignment breeds cynicism and loss of respect.

Advice

Because of your emphasis on results, you won't need to cover with the subordinate every detail required to achieve those results. For example, if you delegate something simple like responsibility for maintaining stocks of office supplies, you won't spend your time telling the person where to order each item. You simply set the goal of keeping adequate supplies at reasonable cost.

However, for more complex delegations, you should advise and direct to make the delegation effective. For example, Barry explains the need for Laura to be persistent in getting the group managers to supply her with the necessary data.

He alerts her to an area where she might run into problems. This type of advice is a proper and necessary part of delegation.

Accountability

Stressing the delegatee's accountability for the task accomplishes two things. First, it makes clear that the ball is in that person's court. It's clear who carries the burden for results. Of course, you're still responsible to your boss for the completion of the task. But your subordinate is accountable to you; you leave no room for confusion about that.

Second, accountability contributes to the person's sense of independence. It gets his or her adrenalin flowing. It provides positive pressure, a shot in the arm, for getting the job done. It motivates.

Along with accountability, you should emphasise that the delegatee is free to make decisions. To some subordinates, this may be a new experience. Make it clear to them that, within certain limits, what they decide in this matter goes.

Dialogue

You'll note from the Barry and Laura dialogue that the process of delegating is not one-sided. Barry does not simply call Laura into his office and give orders. Instead, he encourages her to offer suggestions and comments. He involves her in the process.

Dialogue is an important technique of effective delegation. It draws the subordinate into goals and procedures of the task. It also helps you to spot early potential problems or misunderstandings when they can still be easily corrected. Be sure you get the subordinate to discuss with you the job to be done. When delegatees just listen silently, you don't know if they're getting the message or not.

Acceptance

Always elicit from your subordinate a clear and definite acceptance of the delegated task and the intended results. You want more than murmured approval or tacit acceptance. You want an outright statement that the person agrees on the goals and the deadline. Some managers, especially when delegating a complex project, use a written outline of the task and objectives in order to make sure the delegatee has a crystal-clear idea of exactly what is expected.

Credit

Barry assured Laura that she would receive full credit for her efforts in drawing up the report. This guarantee always helps to motivate the delegatee. It takes on special importance when the subordinate is new to delegation and unsure whether recognition will be forthcoming. Giving credit is an important delegation technique.

Enthusiasm

When you give subordinates new or wider responsibilities, they're likely to feel some trepidation, even fear. It is up to you to boost their enthusiasm, to be a cheerleader. Confidence is contagious. Verbally and by your actions, demonstrate your faith in your subordinates' abilities to overcome obstacles and get results.

Priorities

When approaching delegated assignments, subordinates may feel unsure about what priority to give them in relation to their current duties. Usually, you want to avoid extremes: you don't want delegatees to drop everything and work exclusively on the tasks you're assigning; nor do you want them to feel that they should work on the delegated tasks only in their spare time. Specific deadlines help — they give delegatees flexibility in carrying out their current jobs along with the new ones. You should also find out whether they feel that conflicts with current duties may arise. Try to resolve such conflicts right at the start.

Follow-up

The process of delegation did not end when Laura walked out of Barry's office. Notice that he's already built a follow-up into the assignment. Laura is to notify him immediately if she hasn't gathered tbe bulk of the data in a week. Furthermore, she is to give him a progress report by the fourteenth.

Follow-up is an integral part of the delegation process. Finding the right degree of follow-up — to guide without interfering, to protect against disaster without pampering, to advise without diminishing accountability — is the most subtle aspect of the art of delegation.

The most important aspect of follow-up is control. Checkpoints, progress reports, spending limits, and coaching are all facets of control, which this book covers in depth later on. In summary, techniques of effective delegation include results, time, resources, reasons, some advice, accountability, dialogue, acceptance, credit, enthusiasm, priorities, and follow-up.

Back the subordinate up

Once you pass along to a subordinate the authority and resources to do a job, you must be prepared to back that person up should any legitimate disputes arise with other managers or workers.

For example, Barry had given Laura the authority to examine individual managers' records in compiling the overtime study. One marketing manager told her that he wanted to have the figures typed up before giving them to her. She explained that the original records would be more accurate (no chance for typographical errors) and would give a better idea about how overtime decisions were made. The manager didn't agree and refused to comply.

Laura asked Barry what to do. Barry knew that this manager was particularly cantankerous. Because his overtime record was one of the best in the department, doing it his way wouldn't have seriously marred the study. But because Barry had given Laura the authority to proceed in her own way, he fully supported her request to examine the original figures and made this clear to the recalcitrant manager.

Whose move?

'We've got a problem here.' You've delegated to Joe, one of

your assistants, the task of investigating and correcting manufacturing difficulties that have been holding up shipments on certain products. You run into Joe in the corridor and he makes the above remark. But what does he really mean by 'we'?

'What's the problem?' you ask. He explains. It's not something you want to make a snap judgement about, so you tell him, 'I'll get back to you.' 'We' no longer have a problem. *You* have one. Joe can now rest easily while he waits for you to make a decision.

What has happened? You've delegated an investigation and your subordinate has delegated it back to you. Now it's your move. You can't hold him accountable if he's simply waiting for you to make up your mind.

This shifting back to you of a delegation is something you must always avoid. Subordinates will try it. And when they succeed (as Joe did), they'll continue to try shifting delegations back whenever they encounter sticky situations. In doing this, most subordinates aren't necessarily trying to get out of work. Often, they're genuinely fearful of making decisions. They're just accustomed to leaving the tough questions up to the boss.

The solution to attempts to shift delegations backward is to make the next move his move. 'We've got a problem? Okay, Joe, stop by my office tomorrow with your recommendations on how to handle this situation plus any feasible alternatives.' Now it's his move. And if his solution seems adequate, give him the immediate go-ahead. Still his move. Don't let him shift the accountability on to your shoulders.

Be on the lookout for this tendency among your people to shift back responsibilities. Become an echo. When they ask, 'What do you think?' answer, 'What do *you* think?' If they ask, 'Is that sufficient?' shoot back with, 'Do you think it's sufficient?' 'Is it possible to delay this for a week?' Your answer, 'Is it? Will that meet the goals we've agreed on?'

Forcing delegatees to make the first move is more than a way to keep your own time from being filled up with decisions you've already delegated. It also develops initiative. This delegation technique forces subordinates to grapple with the tough problems rather than rely on help from upstairs. It encourages results-oriented, rather than problem-oriented, thinking.

91

Mistakes

The financial services company that Barry and Laura worked for was partially unionised. About half of the employees in their department were union members. The split was not just between hourly and salaried workers, but was divided along functional lines.

When Barry received Laura's progress report on the over-time study, he noted that she failed to distinguish between union and non-union employees. He knew that this was a significant oversight, which would make questionable the value of her report.

But Barry didn't panic or regret delegating the task. While he didn't expect her to fail in preparing the report, he did know most new delegatees make mistakes. Nor did he call Laura in simply to point out the oversight. He began by praising the thoroughness of her research and the validity of her initial analysis. 'But one thing bothers me, Laura,' he told her. 'Something that we'll have to consider when we tackle overtime costs in the applicable union rules. I'm wondering if your report is going to contribute to that.'

'Maybe it would be better to look at the two groups of workers separately in the study,' Laura suggested. 'I should have thought of that before. It really would make the survey a better working tool for group managers.'

'That's a good approach,' Barry said. 'Can you rework your report in that way and still meet the deadline?'

Laura decided that she could. She went back to work, not stinging from a reprimand or feeling inadequate to the task, but satisfied that she'd spotted her mistake while it could still be rectified.

Remember, too, that people can take only a limited amount of criticism at any one time. When they reach that limit, they become defensive, begin to reject the validity of the criticism, and 'tune out' altogether. When a sub-ordinate really bungles an assignment, try to help him or her iron out the wrinkles piecemeal rather than dumping all the bad news on the person at one time. And mix in a little praise with the bitter medicine to help the person swallow it.

Your attitude

One of the primary qualities of an effective leader is calmness in the face of adversity. Many great military commanders have been noted for the utter coolness with which they faced potential disasters, coolness they conveyed to their officers and men, which prevented panic and needless loss of life. Likewise, outstanding professional athletes usually can block out the hysteria of the crowd and concentrate on the task at hand. This should always be your goal in handling delegation problems. It's not easy, but it will pay off in improved results. Your attitude makes more effective the delegation techniques you use.

Credit and blame

Give your subordinates credit for their successes with delegated tasks. But if they fail, take the blame yourself. Sounds unfair? It is. But it's an important and necessary rule to follow when delegating.

For example, if Laura didn't complete the final draft of her overtime report in time to pass it on to headquarters, Barry shouldn't use as an excuse to his boss the fact that he'd delegated the report to Laura and she'd failed to deliver. While this makes Laura look bad, it tears down Barry's reputation even more. He was responsible for a result — the finished report. If he failed to achieve that result, he shouldn't make excuses. He should simply take steps to correct the situation.

If Barry does lay the blame on her, Laura is likely to feel that she's been made a scapegoat. The project was new to her. She made a sincere effort to do a good job. Now she's being faulted for her efforts. Barry looks bad to both his superiors and his subordinates. To his superiors he appears to duck responsibility; to his subordinates he looks like a manager who doesn't stand behind his people.

Keep in mind, too, that a subordinate's failure may simply mean that you're delegating without following through, that your controls have failed. Proper systems for monitoring subordinates' work will prevent large-scale failures.

As bad as palming off blame on to subordinates is stealing

their glory. It may be true that your advice and guidance contributed a great deal to the person's success. But if you don't let all concerned know that the subordinate deserves the credit, then you're quickly going to run into problems motivating your people.

Why should your subordinates knock themselves out if you are going to bask in the spotlight meant for them? An atmosphere of teamwork is fine. But the coach has to credit his players who perform, not polish his own star.

Delegation do's and dont's

To sum up the process of delegation, here are the 10 most important do's and don'ts to keep in mind when delegating:

Do	Don't
1. Encourage the free flow of information to your subordinates.	Hoard information.
2. Focus on results.	Emphasise methods.
3. Delegate through dialogue.	Do all the talking yourself.
4. Fix firm deadlines.	Leave timescales uncertain.
5. Make sure the person has all necessary resources	Half-delegate by giving assignments without the needed tools.
6. Delegate the entire task to one person.	Delegate half a task.
7. Give advice without interfering.	Fail to point out pitfalls
8. Build controls into the process of delegating	Impose controls as an afterthought.
9. Back up delegatees in legitimate disputes.	Leave people to fight their own battles.
10. Give the delegatee full credit for his or her accomplishments.	Hog the glory or look for scapegoats.

Chapter 6

Obstacles to Effective Delegation

You now have a pretty good grasp of the why, the what, the who, and the how of delegation. But you're still not delegating. Or your efforts aren't producing the results you expect. The purpose of this chapter is to help you identify and overcome the stumbling blocks that every manager encounters in trying to incorporate the power of delegation into his or her management style.

Before you continue reading, take a sheet of paper and jot down some of the reasons you don't delegate or why you aren't reaping the full benefits of delegation. First list the three principal reasons why, in general, you avoid delegating. Next, list the three most common specific reasons that you've given for not delegating a particular task. For example, the first group of reasons might include 'no time available' or 'my people aren't ready for delegation'. Reasons for not delegating specific tasks might be 'too complicated to explain' or 'it's a job I've always done'.

As you proceed through this chapter, glance at the reasons you've jotted down to help keep them in mind. Try to identify the obstacles that are blocking your delegation progress and note on the sheet of paper the ways suggested to overcome them.

Delegation: a tough assignment

No book will ever be written entitled *Delegation Made Easy*. Delegation is not easy. It's complicated, requires hard work, and involves unavoidable risks. Few managers are natural delegators. Each has to learn how to delegate just as each has to learn most managing skills such as listening, motivating, and communicating.

You learn to delegate by first grasping the proper techniques, then recognising and moving beyond specific delegation problems. But more important, you learn by using the skill, by actually delegating. No matter how much theory you get under your belt, you can't become a good delegator if you don't practise, any more than John McEnroe could win at Wimbledon without days spent hitting serves, volleys, lobs, and ground strokes before the tournament begins. It's hard, but look at the rewards! Just imagine doubling or tripling your managerial output over the next year or two. Think what that would do for your pay cheque, for your career, for your self-image.

Delegation stumbling blocks are divided into excuses, obstacles, and resistance. Excuses are those reasons for not delegating that you freely admit. While they may be partly valid, they still block your effectiveness. It's like a marathon runner being stopped by a minor cramp in the foot. Sure it hurts. But is it a valid reason for the runner to give up the entire race? The first step then, in sweeping aside excuses, is to admit that you are using them and to realise that they are just that, excuses.

Obstacles are impediments to delegation. They are roadblocks that you don't create or even see before you bump into them. Organisational obstacles are real problems. For instance, you may have a shared responsibility with another department for getting a job done. You may have to work around that problem in order to delegate in your present job. Personal obstacles consist of attitudes and approaches built into your management style that you didn't know about before you started delegating. They are not overt excuses, but hidden factors that undermine your efforts.

Resistance refers to the reasons why your subordinates fail to cooperate fully in delegation. This is another barrier, but likewise, another one that you can hurdle.

Excuses for failing to delegate effectively

'I can do it better.'
In most cases, it's perfectly true that you can perform the task you want to delegate better than your subordinate could. But always ask yourself, is 'better' necessary?

Remember Shakespeare's advice: 'What will serve is fit.'

For example, a design engineer probably can assemble a complicated machine more quickly and better than a production worker. His intimate knowledge of how the machine works gives him a better feel for the subtleties of the job. But such perfection isn't necessary. And there's no way to justify the cost of an assembly line of trained engineers.

When you spot yourself offering the 'I can do it better' excuse, always counter by asking, 'Can one of my subordinates do an adequate job?' If the person can perform adequately, forget about reaching for better results by doing it yourself. Keep in mind the law of comparative advantage. If all you need is transportation to get you from one place to another, a Ford will do as well as a Rolls Royce.

'I'm afraid my subordinate will fail.'

The possibility of failure haunts some managers and to them seems a logical reason not to risk delegating. They think it's perfectly reasonable and right to be cautious. Since delegating requires them to give up some control and take calculated risks, these managers never delegate.

Two ideas will help you get around this excuse. First, you must realise that calculated risk is both necessary and desirable. Some years ago, the Miller Brewing Co brought out a product that had never sold well before. The company staked a great deal of money on development and marketing. The product, Lite Beer, became an overwhelming success. The risk of entering a new market turned into an advantage. In the same way, the risk that accompanies delegation often pays off in results you'd never otherwise achieve.

Second, you can greatly reduce risks through proper controls. Driving a car entails a certain amount of risk, as motoring fatalities each year glaringly illustrate. But improved brakes, seat belts, and defensive driving lessen most dangers. Delegation doesn't put you into a runaway vehicle, doesn't turn your Talbot into a Formula I. You can still retain control.

'I enjoy doing this task.'

Sure you do. And it feels as comfortable as a well-worn bedroom slipper. But what about results? Where do you want to go in your career? What position would you like to occupy?

Would a person in that position profitably spend his or her time at the type of task you say you enjoy? Is indulging yourself keeping you from leaping over the heads of others for the next available promotion?

'It has to be done right now.'

How can you delegate the task? You need time to get together with your subordinate, talk about results, and start the person on the new task. And your subordinate will take longer to complete it than you would. There's just no time, you think.

Time management is the answer to this excuse. You have to organise your time to delegate. Plan ahead. Don't wait until you're up against the deadline. Take control of your time. Get your priorities straight. Don't bury delegating on the bottom of your 'do' list.

'I don't want my people to think I'm a tyrant.'

Egalitarianism is a persistent theme of modern management thinkers. Some managers are afraid of being too domineering. They worry that their subordinates will think they're dumping work on them just so they can go off to play golf. They're afraid of appearing bossy.

Delegation is not tyranny. Just the opposite in fact. It frees subordinates to decide how to get things done. It lets them participate in setting objectives. When you find yourself using this excuse, practise empathy — put yourself in your people's shoes and consider your delegation from their positions. Then rethink your role in relation to them. Remember that you, like they, must increase your productivity. And for a manager, delegating is the quickest way to improve your personal output.

'I want the credit for these results.'

This selfish excuse indicates that you're suffering from the 'piece of the pie' syndrome. You look on credit and recognition as a pie. If you hand a big slice to your subordinate, there's less left for you. Not so. Delegating increases the size of the pie. Your share of what's left gets bigger. And, your boss will credit both you and your subordinate.

'I want to keep my hand in.'

You're a foreman now, but you can't resist troubleshooting

on the processing equipment. You become the chief accountant, but you find yourself handling some routine bookkeeping. You're sales manager, but you still take care of a few 'special' accounts personally.

Let yourself go. Relax. You've got yourself tied up in a knot. However, delegating means letting go, thinking of priorities. Is keeping your hand in the best way to use your limited time? Almost always it is not.

'I don't want to appear idle.'

Do you think business means 'busy-ness'? Do you feel guilty when you are working at a pace that's less than frantic? Is showing you're working hard more important than getting things done? Do you feel that delegating robs you of your work? There's a famous tale that says oil baron John D. Rockefeller once told a manager, 'You're working too hard. Put your feet up on the desk and think about how Standard Oil can make more money.'

Delegation is a management tool designed to help you get greater results with less effort. Your hectic pace is not a sign of achievement, but of inefficiency. Remember that time spent thinking and planning is a manager's number one duty.

'My boss would want me to handle it personally.'

Sometimes this may be a valid reason not to delegate. But most managers simply use this as an excuse. For example, your boss says, 'I want you to get me a summary of your department's downtime by the tenth.' Does he care how you get the numbers? Or is he interested only in results? Of course it's the results that count.

'I'd rather keep it simple.'

Delegating makes the task more complicated. To avoid the hassle you go ahead and do it yourself. Managers use this excuse to justify not delegating minor tasks. But minor tasks are your best practice ground for developing your delegation skills and habits. Accept the fact that delegation is more complicated. Don't do — delegate.

'I wouldn't ask my people to do anything I'm not willing to do.'

This is the heroic leader fallacy. You want to march at the head of your 'troops'. But consider, for example, someone like a football coach whose success doesn't stem from personal appearances on the field. He leads his team by doing *his* job right: developing strategy and directing his players' efforts. The mark of a true leader is to know his or her role and to do it well, not to engage in heroics.

Organisational obstacles to effective delegation

Obstacle. Understaffed. You have too few people and they're already overworked.
Solution. Apply pressure for a larger staff. If that looks unlikely, get your subordinates to delegate more themselves, either to the people under them or to specialists. Get them to learn time management, too. Cut out unnecessary paperwork and other time wasters. Delegate anyway. Most people can stretch time to handle some additional tasks.

Obstacle. Incompetent hiring. You've simply got the wrong people working for you.
Solution. Make what personnel changes you can. Keep in mind that *every* subordinate can take on some delegations, if only limited ones.

Obstacle. Poor training and promotion. Your subordinates have moved up too quickly. They aren't ready.
Solution. It's up to you. The situation calls for a great deal of patience, close guidance, tight controls, and a programme of gradual delegation. Remember that delegation is the best form of training. Shape the delegation and accompanying controls to the subordinate's current level of competence and skill.

Obstacle. Organisational confusion. Example: your boss skips over you and assigns work to your subordinates. That's about as welcome as castor oil in a chocolate factory. It makes effective delegation much more difficult.
Solution. Take your boss aside. Have him or her fully define your duties and those of the people on your staff in the form of job descriptions. If you already have them, make sure your boss sticks to the organisational tracks the job descriptions lay out. Be extra careful, when delegating tasks, to make clear that your delegatee is accountable to you. Giving

clear priorities and deadlines also lessens organisational confusion.

Obstacle. Organisational stagnation. Just the opposite of organisational confusion. The organisational chart is carved in stone. All directives come down from 'on high'. Top managers greet initiatives with frowns.
Solution. Make the best of the situation. Delegate prudently and keep a log of results to back up your decisions and to show the doubters. Pay particular attention to controls. Give your people freedom to carry out delegated tasks, but make them keep in close touch with you so that you can answer to your own boss for their actions.

Obstacle. Instability. No one wants to take chances because of uncertainty in the organisation. People protect their turfs like a mother hen protects her chicks. This situation develops when financial problems cause layoffs. At such times employees resist delegations because they fear that their current, familiar jobs are less secure.
Solution. Pick delegations that are closely related to your subordinates' current job functions. For example, have a quality control inspector oversee experiments with reworking defective parts. Make your people understand that new skills acquired from tackling new tasks will increase their security, not undermine their current positions.

Obstacle. Delegation devalued. This kind of company pushes its managers to burn the midnight oil rather than delegate to subordinates. Management ignores the ability to delegate, doesn't credit it in performance evaluations. How things have always been done, and who has done them, are considered all-important.
Solution. You'll have to slash your own way through this kind of jungle. Delegate, get results, and show the company the cause-and-effect relationship. Have a frank discussion with your boss. Chances are, he or she is a 'doer' and has stuck to that approach. Sell your boss the reasons you want to delegate. Be sure of your controls and proceed step by step.

Personal obstacles to effective delegation

Obstacle. Delegation is difficult. You're not likely to admit, even to yourself, that the reason you don't delegate is because it's just plain hard. But, in fact, many managers shy away from delegating because it doesn't feel right to them, they aren't comfortable when they delegate.

Solution. Recognise that delegation is not an instinct. It's a skill that you learn and develop. Build up gradually to delegating until you acquire a feel for the method. Delegate trivia first. Pass on a few of those minor routine tasks. Don't kid yourself that 'I'm just not a delegator'. If you're a manager, you're a delegator — or should be.

Obstacle. You love action. Most managers do. And action often involves you in tasks that you should delegate. A good example is the sales manager whose mouth waters when he thinks about getting out into the field and closing deals.

Solution. Re-evaluate your role as a manager. Are you really alive to the responsibilities and potentials of your job? Or are you marking time, filling in as a cog in the machine? Management has its own excitement and rewards for the true manager.

For example, the sales manager should stop looking at himself simply as an administrator. He should delegate more of those duties and focus increasingly on such functions as planning, developing new selling techniques, and turning losing salesmen into winners.

Obstacle. You're uncertain of your own authority. For example, you're the office manager of a large law firm. The firm has recently purchased a minicomputer and hired a programmer-operator. You've been looking into upgrading the word processing system and would like to investigate the feasibility of linking it to the computer. You would like to delegate certain studies and evaluations to the programmer. But you're uncertain whether your authority as office manager covers the situation. You don't delegate and try to do it all yourself.

Solution. Go to your boss and find out how much authority you have. Try to get a general description of your limits of authority or you'll find yourself running back to your boss to ask about your authority on every job you want to delegate.

When in doubt, delegate. Take a chance. Don't be too cautious. Sometimes you have to bet all your chips on a throw of the dice. At times you must seize authority rather than sit silently waiting for it to be granted. If, as the office manager, you take the initiative and delegate to the computer programmer to get specific results, your action can hardly be faulted.

Obstacle. You're an autocrat. You won't admit it, but look at the way you operate: you constantly give orders, thus coaching your people to wait for them. You motivate through fear, so your people spend a good deal of time covering their backs. You give them the impression, 'Do it my way or you're fired,' to quote the title of a book by David Ewing, managing editor of the *Harvard Business Review.* So they never display initiative. You think you're tough and hard-headed, but in reality you're rigid and narrow-minded.

Solution. Don't define this obstacle in terms of good guy v bad guy. Forget whether you're a pal to your people, or whether they view you as an ogre. Instead, focus on results, which are what really count in the end. You don't have to win a popularity contest, but you do have to get things done. And a delegation style beats a crack-the-whip style every time.

Ironically, one of the reasons managers often develop into autocrats is that they don't use controls properly. Delegation never implies abandonment. Use control methods that will let you give responsibility to your subordinates but still keep you in close touch with what is happening.

Obstacle. You can't communicate. 'This isn't exactly what I had in mind. I can't explain it, but I'll know it when I see it.' That statement is a symptom of poor communication. Do you find yourself saying something similar? Delegation requires you to communicate clearly both the results that you want and the information the person will need to get the job done. Remember, you have a 'data bank' stored in your head, which your subordinate cannot automatically tap into. Your experience gives you knowledge, instincts, and feelings that guide your approach to any task. But trying to articulate these ideas can be as tricky as juggling four balls at one time. So, rather than delegate, you go ahead and tackle the job yourself.

Solution. Communication is easier when properly structured. Organise your thoughts into categories before you talk with the delegatee. Classify the task according to results, resources, and controls. Handle each topic in order. Jot down notes of the points you want to make. Remember to listen. Listening is the better half of communicating. It informs you of what your subordinate is trying to say and guides you as to how to clarify your own remarks. Also, keep up a constant information flow. The more your people pick up from day to day, the less specific information they'll need when you're making a delegation.

Obstacle. You've failed at delegation. A subordinate lets you down after you entrusted that person with an important assignment. Now you 'know' that delegation isn't worth the effort.

Solution. Experience doesn't always teach the right lesson. A cat that sits on a hot stove learns, and never sits on a hot stove again. But it never sits on a cold one, either. Keep in mind the following points:

- Delegating can, at times, fail to produce the results expected.
- Controls minimise the chances of disaster.
- The best managers are effective delegators.
- Any manager can learn to delegate, but it takes practice.

Obstacle. Interpersonal contact makes you uncomfortable. You're aloof, don't like working closely with people. Handing out orders eliminates the necessary discussion and give-and-take of delegation. You prefer it that way.

Take, for example, the case of an accountant for a large computer service company. This woman was an excellent financial analyst. She excelled at her work and received two quick promotions. Suddenly, she found herself supervising a staff of 12 other accounting specialists. But she found it very hard to make contact with her subordinates, to 'reach out and touch someone'. She couldn't get to know them or their capabilities. She vacillated between answering, 'I'll handle it myself' and issuing orders without any preliminary discussion or agreement on goals. She became a workaholic, isolated from her people — who then lost their motivation.

Solution. The solution to this one is about as easy as skiing up an icy slope. Attack the problem one step at a time. Make yourself take a course such as one from Dale Carnegie.

That will make you do something with other people. Ask your boss for outside training. Seminars that investigate group dynamics can be helpful, so can assertiveness training. Talk over the problem with your boss and with other more experienced managers. They will be able to give you practical advice for breaking through your reluctance to deal with other people. Then, start delegating small tasks on the job and work up to major ones. Pay careful attention to the correct delegation techniques as described in Chapter 4.

Obstacle. You don't trust your people. You feel they're slackers who will slide into idleness without strict supervision. You think some are incompetent. Whatever the concern, you don't want to take a chance on them by delegating.

Solution. The management theorist Rufus E. Miles, Jr put this obstacle into a nutshell: 'Freedom to make good decisions,' he said, 'means freedom to make bad decisions.' Controls help to limit the consequences of those bad decisions. But, in the end, you have to take a chance on your people. All managers take risks — or they don't remain managers for long. You have to trust subordinates. The next chapter discusses ways of building mutual trust.

Obstacle. Envy. You avoid delegating to key subordinates, not because you're afraid they'll fail, but because you dread seeing them succeed. You worry that they will show you up. You chafe at the fact that a young company phenomenon is skyrocketing to the top while your own progress has been hard won. You delegate trivial duties to the person, but you hold back the type of delegation that would give him or her a chance to really shine.

Solution. Self-interest. Think of your department or unit as a team. What do you need in order to earn recognition? Achievement. Spectacular results. Your job is to direct and lead all of your people toward those results. Everyone on a team profits when the team wins the league championship, especially the leader, the quarterback. And they win by contributing their maximum potentials.

Delegating to develop younger managers pays additional dividends. An administrative manager at one of the major automobile companies was famous inside the company for the number of promising managers who'd passed through his department. 'Don't you find it frustrating,' he was asked, 'to develop competent subordinates only to have them promoted out of your department?' 'Not at all,' he replied. 'To get things done in a large organisation like this, you need allies. Every person who's been promoted away from me gives me another ally. And the higher they move in the company, the more valuable they become to me.'

Resistance to delegation

So you've put aside your excuses and crashed through the obstacles. You're ready and willing to delegate. Trouble is, your people don't want to go along. They don't jump with joy over taking on new tasks. They drag their feet, greeting your delegating ideas with the same enthusiasm they show when stepping into the dentist's chair.

To a certain extent, this may be the result of novelty. If you're a new manager or supervisor or haven't delegated much thus far, your people may be justifiably wary of your efforts to suddenly involve them in setting goals and making decisions. Best to proceed surely but gradually, like the tortoise in the old fable of the hare and the tortoise. Clarify your ideas of delegation as you extend the scope of your delegating. As subordinates see the advantages to them in the process, their resistance will vanish. In those cases where certain subordinates continue to resist your attempts to delegate tasks to them, pin down the cause and overcome it. Managing, after all, is the art of getting things done through people by means of persuasion; only when persuasion fails do you use command.

Overcoming reluctance of delegatees

Reluctance to accept delegated tasks often stems from delegatees' lack of self-confidence. They are afraid to risk failure. These subordinates always see assignments as too much of a challenge. They fear they haven't the skills or experience necessary for the job. They think they're being hit with too much too soon.

106

Fashioning a series of successes is the best way to handle these cases, like setting up easy fights first when developing a boxer. Each new delegation should help to build up confidence for the next one. Spend more time with such persons, reviewing your controls over their actions to handle the tasks. But don't allow these subordinates to lean on you. Make it a point to express clearly your confidence in their abilities.

Reluctance can also be a symptom of laziness. That's a far tougher problem to overcome. Calling a person lazy gets the same reaction as waving a red flag before the snout of a bull. When you've come to the end of your rope in trying to get such employees to accept responsibility and you know they are lazy, you have no recourse. Replace them, or give them structured jobs where they can vegetate for the rest of their careers.

Overcoming uncertainty

Some subordinates resist delegation because they are unsure of the situation. Here are four examples of this type of attitude:

'Do I have the authority?'

Nothing is more likely to cause uncertainty about taking on new duties than to have been given an assignment without enough authority to carry it out. For example, as plant manager you delegate to a department supervisor the task of implementing certain cost-cutting measures. This means the person will have to issue orders to other department supervisors and make sure they are carried out. Questions about authority immediately come up. Will the other supervisors resist someone who is only an equal? When push comes to shove, are you going to make the supervisor's authority clear and back it up? It's no wonder that uncertainty about authority can cause resistance to delegations.

You must be very clear and firm about the extent of the authority you're passing on to subordinates. Don't assume they know what their authority is. Spell it out. Make it explicit. And make sure that it's sufficient to get the job done.

'Will I receive credit?'
Why make the effort and have someone else steal the glory? That's an understandable attitude for persons who aren't accustomed to taking on delegated tasks,. duties, or responsibilities. When you delegate to your subordinates, they take risks just as you do. They must make decisions. They must supply initiative. In return, they can rightfully expect to get credit for their successes. If they don't, they're going to be uncertain about accepting the next assignment.

Oral recognition, a letter of commendation with copies to higher-up managers, a chance to sit in on a meeting with higher management, a rise or bonus, a more favourable work station or office, an opportunity to take breaks at will, or even the much joked about key to the executives' washroom, all can serve as credit for doing the delegated tasks successfully. Going public with recognition, making sure you don't steal any subordinates' thunder, makes delegatees seek out new worlds to conquer and eliminates any reluctance or uncertainty about their accepting new delegations as you pass them along.

'Do I have the facts?'
Imagine walking through a fully furnished living room in the pitch dark. One wrong move and you've cracked your shin against a coffee table or reduced a Ming vase to fragments. How would you proceed? Not at all if you could help it. Very, very carefully, otherwise.

Then think of the state of mind of a subordinate who's just been handed a formidable task, made accountable for results, given a strict deadline, but is almost completely unaware of the facts surrounding the assignment.

An earlier chapter discussed the value of a continual flow of information to subordinates to keep them up to speed for delegations. The marketing director of a small consumer products firm kept a 'facts of life' file in his office. Into it went letters, memos, reports, statistics, summaries of competitors' activities, industry surveys, brochures, magazines and newspaper articles — anything he found potentially useful to his job. He made his key subordinates review the 'facts of life' once a week. This kept them nearly as well informed on useful internal and external facts as the manager himself. When he delegated, he could assume a high level of background knowledge. The technique gave subordinates greater confidence in accepting delegations because they felt they had more background to understand a given assignment. It made delegating quicker and easier for the marketing director, too.

'I've heard this before.'
Subordinates who have dropped the ball when you've passed along delegated tasks in the past often become unnerved and resist other assignments. They're afraid that another fumble will demote them permanently. Choose tasks for these people that are well within their capabilities. Go into a confidence-building routine as suggested before by fashioning a series of successes.

Overcoming bad habits

Resistance to delegation can bubble up not only from reluctance or uncertainty, but simply from bad habits. Employees quickly fall into such habits in work situations where delegation is rare.

The 'please the boss' syndrome
Results take a back seat to the things your people imagine you 'really' want. They constantly test you with trial balloons to try and gauge your true feelings. They press you to tell them how to perform a task, rather than working independently within the controls you've set up. They frequently seek your approval. The please-the-boss syndrome works against the advantages of delegation, which include subordinates bringing you solutions and results, not questions and problems. Often managers are at fault, not their people. They don't require subordinates to take risks or make decisions. Ask yourself these questions if your people display this syndrome:

- Do I really talk about results I want rather than methods?
- Do I discourage my people when they ask for advice they don't really need?
- Do I turn back their questions to them, forcing them to tell me what course they'll take before I comment?

- Do I take back tasks too quickly before making every effort to keep the subordinate accountable?

The 'you're the greatest' ploy

This is a variation on the 'please-the-boss' syndrome. Subordinates play on the manager's ego, pride, and expertise. 'You're the expert on this type of stress analysis, Mr Jones. I can't handle it the way you can. What should I do?' 'You're the best cost accountant in the company, Jane. Tell me how to allocate these costs.' Such strategems are about as subtle as a kick on the shins. Yet some managers are so flattered that they forgo good delegation techniques to bask in their subordinates' esteem. Be alert for this type of ploy. Counter such questions by saying, 'I think you'd better learn where to find that kind of information in case you need it when I'm not around.' Or, 'I learned cost accounting by doing it. I think you should, too.'

No time to say 'hello'

Some of your people resist delegated tasks because they're 'too busy'. Few people in office jobs are overworked. Many others, even in glamour jobs like airline pilots, are protected by contracts. More likely they waste time, manage their time poorly, and don't delegate to their own subordinates.

You can't do much with contract people. That's a job for your labour negotiator. Basically, you have a selling job to do on what's in it for them to become a cooperative delegatee. That's a subject well covered in earlier chapters, which you should review when this problem comes up.

The problem of overdelegation

The manager of the West Country sales office of a paper products company had a very competent assistant. He delegated tasks to the assistant and was very pleased with the results. Gradually, he delegated more and more of his duties. He found that he didn't need to come to the office until late morning and could leave early. He rubber-stamped the assistant's actions, signed the necessary forms, talked to his sales reps from time to time, but eventually gave over most of the running of the office to the assistant.

Wasn't this manager simply following the rule to 'delegate everything'? Didn't he clear a great deal of his time for planning? What exactly was wrong? This manager made several errors. Delegating too many tasks wasn't the problem.

The sales manager failed to use properly one of the great advantages of delegation — free time. He neglected to take on the policy and planning roles his job required. While the office ran smoothly, he was not planning future directions, uncovering new markets, or improving sales techniques. In the end, he became so far out of touch with day-to-day operations that he couldn't handle these important managerial duties anyway.

Overdelegation sometimes means that you've delegated some jobs that you should do yourself. For example, a customer complaint manager of a large department store called together her staff to discuss better approaches to dealing with the public. A number of proposals were put forward. At the end of the meeting, the manager said, 'I think this has been a fruitful discussion. I urge you all to go back and put these ideas into practice as you see fit.'

This manager was delegating policy decisions that she should have handled herself. The clerks should not have been left to decide company policy on such issues as refunds, returned merchandise, credit, and cheque cashing. In fact, each clerk might come up with policies that conflict or differ from customer to customer. A clear case of overdelegation. Review Chapter 3, which covers tasks that are not appropriate to delegate. Be careful to apply the tests to each assignment you make. Is it policy? A specific personnel matter? Confidential?

Another symptom of overdelegation crops up when you give subordinates assignments that demand too much of them or for which they can never be trained. Try to strike a balance. Delegation should challenge, it should stretch, but it should not make people reach beyond their longest grasp. Take careful note of the person's skills, experience, and potentials. While unfamiliar tasks always require extra effort, no one has yet been able to turn lead into gold — but not for lack of trying!

Any delegation can become overdelegation if you neglect proper controls. Later chapters discuss this question in detail. Just remember that no matter how much you delegate, you can never relieve yourself of the ultimate responsibility for results.

Chapter 7

The Psychology of Delegation

Sam Brown was production supervisor for a power tool manufacturer. His company planned to introduce a new product, a battery-powered compressor. Production schedules and logistics needed to be set up. In addition, someone would have to track the product through its early stages of production to work out any snags that developed. As he was wrapped up in his ordinary duties, Sam thought this would be a good opportunity to delegate.

He called in his assistant manager, Pete Rogers, and told him that he would be given production responsibility for the compressor. The two men had been working closely together, so Pete already had a good idea of what the job involved. He said he felt confident in tackling it. They talked over the goals of the task, speculated about potential problems, set up deadlines, and agreed on the controls that would keep Sam posted on progress.

This was a properly delegated task. Both the preparation and execution of the delegation were carried out smoothly. But now let's take a look inside Sam Brown's head after Pete left his office. We find a stew of conflicting emotions:

- *Guilt.* 'Pete already has his hands full. This new assignment will probably work him to death.'
- *Fear.* 'What if Pete really blows it? That'll look bad for me, too. I'll have to take the blame. I could lose my job.'
- *Envy.* 'But Pete's a sharp guy. What if he succeeds too well? That'll make me look bad by comparison.'
- *Anxiety.* 'I wish I were handling this myself. I just don't feel right about it. I know *something* will go wrong.'
- *Distrust.* 'Maybe Pete will purposely try to make me look bad. What does he really think?'
- *Conflict.* Sam's boss called him up the next day and said

that marketing wanted to get the compressor out a week earlier than the original plan called for. Sam agreed it could be done. But then he felt torn between accommodating his boss and putting more pressure on his subordinate.

Even though he was an experienced delegator, Sam fell victim to these emotions. But because of his experience, he didn't allow any of them to panic him. He dealt with them, letting Pete go ahead with the task. As a result, the new product rolled off the assembly line without a hitch.

Delegation and stress

This case illustrates an important fact about delegation: it's no bed of roses. Guilt, fear, envy, anxiety, conflict, distrust, plus the inevitable frustrations you'll encounter as you monitor your subordinate's progress, add a dash of deadline pressure, and the result is stress. How do you eliminate the stress connected with delegating? You don't. You can lessen it. You can learn to live with it. But you cannot get rid of it unless you give up delegating altogether. It's part of the price of being a manager.

Just as any problem loses some of its ferocity the closer you examine it, a look at some of the components of delegation stress will help you to tame this monster.

Guilt

Go back and review Chapter 2, 'Why Delegate?'. In a nutshell, effective delegation benefits everyone: you, your subordinate, and your organisation. While Sam was feeling guilty about burdening his assistant, Pete Rogers might have been celebrating his good fortune at being handed added responsibility.

Fear

Fear often shrivels under the light of close examination. First, admit that you're worried. You have every right to be. Next, pin down what you're specifically worried about — the worst possible outcome. Finally, analyse the fear realistically. For example, fear makes Sam's thoughts jump to the possibility of losing his job — the worst possible outcome. But careful analysis shows him that, no matter how badly things go with this one project, this outcome is very, very unlikely.

Next, he decides that the worst possible outcome is a severe reprimand that might hurt his career. Realistic evaluation: given the controls he's set up, Pete's competence and experience, and his own boss's understanding of the need to develop managers through delegation, this outcome, too, is so unlikely that it's not worth a second thought. In the end, Sam decides that the worst outcome he need seriously consider — a major production problem that would take some long hours to straighten out — isn't much to be afraid of. It's unlikely, to begin with. He can handle it if it occurs. His fear subsides.

Envy

The trouble with this emotion is that it's often hidden. Some managers refrain from giving particular subordinates tasks because they say they don't think those subordinates can handle the responsibilities. What they really mean is, they're afraid they can handle them only too well.

Begin by rooting out this emotion. Question your repeated refusal to delegate challenging tasks to a subordinate. Next, look to your own self-interest. Can you obtain something good by the person's success? You'll find that your envy has no rational foundation. It vanishes. You see that your profit from successful delegation will be at least as great as that of your subordinate.

Anxiety

Anxiety is fear of the unknown. You feel worried and apprehensive, but you can't say exactly why. Because you are unable to pinpoint the object of your anxiety, as you can the object of your fear, anxiety is harder to dispel. Remember, though, that some anxiety is good. It makes you alert and observant, keeps you on your toes. Also, anxiety may be a warning signal that you've left something undone. Is your subordinate really ready for the assignment? Are the controls you've put in place adequate? A careful review of the way in which you've followed the

115

techniques of delegating may help to ease some of your excess anxiety.

Conflict

Sometimes, you feel as if you're caught in a vice, between a rock and a hard place. A subordinate explains that he needs another few days to finish a task you've delegated to him. You think his argument is reasonable. Your boss, though, wants it done 'yesterday, if not sooner'. Because you've delegated, you're the one in the middle.

Here's a chance to earn your pay as a manager. Sometimes, you'll have to play the diplomat, urging your boss to be patient while you build a fire under your subordinates to step up their efforts. Other times, you'll have to defend your subordinates staunchly, protecting them against pressure from above. You've agreed on a deadline and a change in midstream would disrupt the delegation process. The success of both this and future delegations depends on your backing the person up. This may make you feel as comfortable as the guy who was given the job of loading ten tons of canaries in a five-ton truck. He got the job done but only by having some delegatee bang the top of the truck with a baseball bat to keep half of the canaries in the air all the time. But then, who said managing was easy?

Trust: the bedrock of delegation

All delegation is built on a foundation of trust. But trust is far from being a simple psychological process. It can take years to establish, or be destroyed in an instant. Trust puts demands on both manager and subordinate to reach beyond themselves. It doesn't require agreement or even a cordial relationship. But you can't substitute for it, you can't feign it, you can't buy it. It must be earned.

Both trust and distrust feed on themselves. 'The only way to make a man trustworthy is to trust him, and the surest way to make him untrustworthy is to distrust him and show your distrust,' is the way American statesman Henry Stimson put it.

The figure on page 117 shows how both trust and distrust

The spirals of trust and distrust

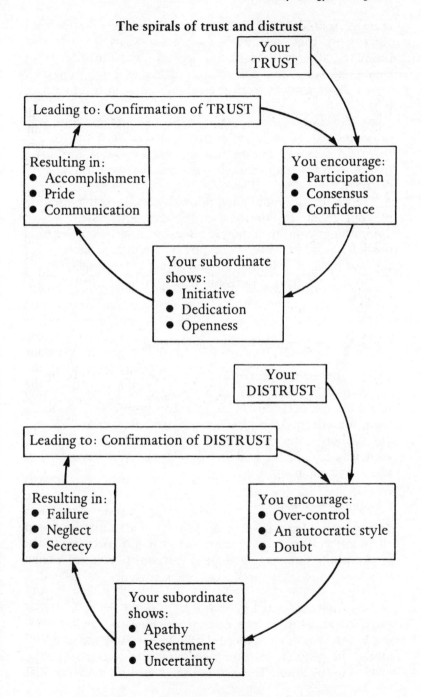

are represented as spirals. Too often, managers 'know' they can't trust their people. They see the signs in their subordinates' displays of apathy, secrecy, and hostility. What they don't see is that the situation stems as much from their own lack of trust as from the subordinates' innate incorrigibility.

As the figure shows, your trust encourages your subordinates so that they get results that confirm your trust in them. Conversely, your distrust encourages your subordinates to act in ways that result in failures, thus confirming your distrust.

Trust does not imply blind faith, though. It isn't a question of your giving up control. Nor of being softheaded. Nor of diminishing your own power. Because it makes delegation possible, trust increases your power. Because it discourages the hoarding of information and clears away doubts about motives, trust frees an organisation to achieve greater effectiveness.

Some proven methods for enhancing trust

Says management expert Rufus E Miles, 'Either you make up your mind that you, as a manager, will have a certain tolerance for decisions made in a way you would not make them, or you make no important delegations at all.' Accept your subordinates' methods. Insisting on things being done your way nips in the bud any developing trust between you and your people.

Backstop their decisions

Though you don't have to agree with your subordinates at all times, you must never leave them hanging to twist slowly in the wind. Your people depend on you. If you don't back them up when they need you, their trust in you is undermined.

Take the case of a buyer at a large retail chain. She delegated to an assistant the task of stocking up certain items for a forthcoming promotion. While she and the assistant agreed in general on the objectives, she left the specific quantities to him. The promotion was so successful that more goods were sold than the assistant had bought for stock. When the director of merchandising complained about the stockouts to the buyer, she said, 'I left that entirely up to George. You'd better ask him.' How well did George perform in future delegations? Will he be eager for further decision-making responsibility?

Don't harp on mistakes

Mistakes speak loudly. Success is often quiet. Once subordinates recognise that they made errors, don't rub it in. Emphasise the positive. Find something they did right and compliment them. Then correct and demonstrate how the errors could have been avoided. In the same way, focus on efforts, not circumstances. For example, if a subordinate works out what you know is an excellent proposal only to have it arbitrarily rejected by a client, make sure that you give the person proper credit and pats on the back anyway.

Don't spy on subordinates

Where is the line between spying and simply checking up? It's not easy to find. Is making discreet enquiries among fellow workers, about how a person is getting on, spying? Or checking? You should be careful about how you handle such a situation. When possible, check directly with your subordinate. One thing is sure: assigning someone specifically to keep watch over a subordinate begins the cycle of distrust.

Don't withhold information as a test

Take this example. A personnel manager asked his assistant to look into the background of a man applying for a job as an engineer. With considerable digging, the assistant determined that the applicant had falsified some of his academic qualifications. He wrote up a report for his boss, thinking he'd done a good job. When he pointed out the information, the manager replied, 'Yes, I know he faked that degree. I just wanted to see if you'd catch it.'

Some managers think this type of one-upmanship keeps subordinates on their toes. It doesn't. It tears down the trust needed for effective delegation. Subordinates should begin

119

any delegated task feeling that, as far as possible, they have all the facts that you do. Withholding information keeps them wondering, keeps them from trusting you fully.

Be open

Let your subordinates see your human side. You make mistakes. Some of your brainstorms turn out to be so much rainwater. You become peeved. You act as though you got up on the wrong side of the bed some mornings. Letting your feelings out into the open — without, of course, letting them get the better of you — shows your people that you're the real thing, that you're human. They feel they can trust you because they know you.

Openness is particularly important when you're dealing directly with subordinates. If you are angry, frustrated, disappointed, elated — let it show. They're going to sense your feelings from your attitude and body language anyway. If you cover up, they'll never be sure exactly what you feel. A person who occasionally blows up inspires far more trust than one who just smoulders all the time. And your reactions to events go over better if they're fairly predictable. When you explode one time over a mistake and next time take it with a grin, that makes life tough on your subordinates. They never know what to expect. You have to try to react to the same events in the same way while still being human.

Clarify your expectations

Let your people know what you expect in advance. Communicate. Make sure you're both speaking the same language before you delegate. Trust cannot be built on the basis of post mortems or irregular spurts of activity. A clear sense of what is expected contributes to mutual trust.

Show respect

Trust requires you to exercise simple courtesy. Don't stand on the empty forms of authority or status. Saying 'please' and phrasing orders in the form of requests are basics. Making a statement like, 'Reword this report, it sounds lousy,' may elicit the same results as saying, 'This report looks good, but do you think you could reword it to make it read better?' But the second attitude contributes to trust, while the first undermines it. Likewise, don't lean on the prerogatives of your position. Don't keep subordinates standing while you sit. Don't make them wait unnecessarily for an 'audience'. Don't needlessly interrupt. Don't 'pull rank' to gratify your own ego.

Don't manipulate

Somebody has to clean the latrines. But consider the boss who calls in his subordinate and says, 'Al, we're going to promote you to chief sanitary engineer. No pay rise, but you'll have a great opportunity to get around the whole plant. Here's your mop.' Al's mental reply to this type of manipulative assignment wouldn't be fit to print. And it surely wouldn't show more trust in his boss. 'Busy' work, petty restrictions introduced solely to discipline subordinates, and secrecy about matters that are important to the company are all forms of manipulation. Be honest and keep the information flowing.

Examine assumptions

Do you ever find yourself thinking the following:

- 'People always look for the easiest way out.'
- 'They don't know what they really want.'
- 'They don't realise what's good for them.'
- 'Left to themselves, most workers are lazy.'

These are a few of the assumptions that can get in the way of trust. If you think your subordinates are simply looking for the easiest way out of any situation, how far can you trust them when you delegate? These are exactly the types of assumption that become self-fulfilling prophecies. Remember the spirals of trust and distrust.

The same kinds of assumption apply to individuals. If you hang a label on each of your subordinates — one is 'lazy', one's a 'troublemaker', another's 'sloppy' — then you are going to react to the label and not to the person. This tears down trust and makes delegation much more difficult.

Personal style affects delegating

When you recognise that individual styles of operating affect delegating, you'll be able to improve your delegation effectiveness. Take the case of the manager of a trucking company who was complaining about one of his despatchers: 'Every time I give Dave an assignment, he always protests that he's not up to it, he doesn't have the skills or expertise. And yet, so far, he's had very few problems on any tasks I've delegated to him.'

'I know,' the manager's colleague said. 'That's just the way Dave is. Doesn't seem to have much self-confidence, but gets the job done. All he needs is reassurance.'

Every subordinate must be treated as an individual. Some are naturally argumentative. Some are deeply analytical: they won't agree it's Thursday until they look at the calendar, then check to make sure it's this year's calendar. Some act on impulse, others want all the facts. Some have an easy time making up their minds, others decide only after agonizing over the contingencies. Some people are moved by appeals to reason, others respond primarily to emotions.

The worst thing you can do is to lump all your people into a single category and use the same managing style on each one. For some subordinates, you'll have to lay out the facts in precise order and show them where they're going and why. Others need only a general overview of the situation, but then have to be spurred to action by your enthusiasm and emotional involvement.

Remember, too, that you have your own management style, one that comes naturally to you. You'll have to learn to vary it to fit the individual and the situation. If you tend to be emotional, make sure you don't go overboard. If you're as cool as a cucumber, you've got to get some fire into your act to inspire when needed. When a tornado hits, you may have to be autocratic and order everybody to get down to the basement. When you're planning the company dinner dance, you can be democratic in your style. Pay attention to facts and analysis, too. If you're an extremely decisive type, try to avoid stepping on your subordinates' toes. Let them make their own decisions. If you go in for detail, don't lose sight of the big picture when delegating to your people.

According to Robert Heller in his book *The Super-managers*, at Texas Instruments the two big bosses took their eyes off the big picture. They paid too much attention to details like computer rankings of every operating manager. Over-control occurred in a company noted for its innovation from the bottom up and contributed to two huge failures in a span of a few years: digital watches and home computers. They couldn't see the forest for the trees.

Motivating: what do subordinates want?

A survey conducted by the US Labor Relations Institute among more than 10,000 employees and supervisors produced some interesting findings. Employees were asked which job factors they considered most important. Supervisors were asked which factors they thought employees looked on as important. The supervisors listed 'good wages' as the most vital consideration for their people, followed by 'job security'. The workers, on the other hand, ranked 'full appreciation of work done' as the most important factor, with 'a feeling of being in on things' number two.

What this survey indicates is that many managers have a mistaken notion about what really motivates their people. Famed psychologist Abraham Maslow suggested that the needs that motivate people could be ranked. He listed them in this order:

1. Bodily needs (food and shelter)
2. Safety (freedom from danger)
3. Belonging (being part of a group)
4. Esteem (status and achievement)
5. Self-actualisation (insight into one's nature).

Maslow stated that the more basic needs motivate a person first. When the basic needs are satisfied, the higher needs begin to motivate. A hungry man is not likely to work too hard to win a good citizenship award. First, he's going to look for something to eat. Having found a secure supply of food, that need no longer motivates him; rather, the need for safety becomes his primary motivation. Once secure, belonging takes over as the primary motivator, and so on up the hierarchy.

Supervisors, then, tend to look on the lower needs as being important to their people. Wage levels and job security fall into the general area of bodily needs and safety. But what workers say is important to them — appreciation and being in on things — fits into the higher needs of belonging and esteem. This is good news for managers approaching delegation. Their employees' primary needs for sustenance and safety have been satisfied. Delegation appeals directly to people's needs for esteem and belonging, a higher need on Maslow's pyramid, and one that now motivates because the lower needs are satisfied. You, as a delegator, should keep these concepts of motivation in mind when you consider the psychology of the process.

Defining the job

One way you can put Maslow's hierarchy to work motivating your people lies in the way you define their jobs. Compare, for example, how two different supervisors begin delegating to a subordinate the task of reviewing quality control procedures:

Manager A. 'Head office wants another one of these quality control reports. I don't know why. You'll have to go around to each inspection station and note the procedures used on all the products that come through.'

Manager B. 'Our customers are especially interested in quality. And in today's market, it means a lot to the company to have a reputation for high quality. What I think we can do here is to find ways to improve quality control by reviewing the current procedures.'

What's the difference? Manager *A* appeals to neither belonging nor achievement. He doesn't represent the task as part of a joint effort by the entire company to put out quality products, but rather as another order that's come down from 'head office'. He doesn't emphasise the results that the subordinate is to achieve, but starts right off on the method. The only motivation he provides is the implicit threat of a reprimand if the task isn't completed satisfactorily.

Manager *B*, with a few words, presents the same assignment

in an entirely different light. First, he lets the subordinate know why the task is an important one. He puts it in the context of the mutual efforts of everyone in the company. Then he points out specific results that the person can aim at and achieve. His subordinate will be doubly motivated: first, to seek the esteem and status that results from achieving an important objective; second, to feel pride from participating in the teamwork of the firm, polishing the company's reputation in the process.

The role in involvement one company plays

Many companies in recent years have recognised the value of giving their workers a broader view of the significance of their jobs and of their role in the overall functioning of the company. Their efforts to involve employees through more thorough communication and participation have paid off by building a pool of motivation on which managers can draw, particularly when making delegations.

Pitney Bowes Inc, the largest manufacturer of postage meters, believes that superior communications makes its personnel more effective in everything they do, including delegating and carrying out delegations. Each spring the US company holds a series of Job Holder Meetings, first at headquarters and then at its plants and offices. Every officer, manager, and employee gets a chance to attend one such meeting.

The meetings are conducted by officers of Pitney Bowes and a panel of elected employees called the Council of Personnel Relations (CPR). Each meeting starts with a brief presentation of company results during the past year and plans for the future. Then the meetings are thrown open for a two- to two-and-a-half-hour period of questions from the floor. Questions may range from those about food in the cafeteria to salaries. Employees can submit in writing before the meeting any question to the CPR. *All* questions will be answered. However, any that are personally embarrassing to an individual will be answered outside the meeting if the questioner has signed his or her name to the submission form.

For questions that come up that neither the officers present nor the CPR can answer at the meeting because the facts aren't readily available, the company publishes 'Getting Back to You', which is distributed to employees. To further improve the flow of information, the CPR meets every two months to hold departmental meetings.

When we asked the purpose of such meetings, one employee replied enthusiastically, 'It's good communications and gives you a chance to air your views.' It's a top-down and bottom-up communications technique that lets everyone in the company operate in an environment where an open flow of information is the norm, not the exception. Such an environment promotes better results from managers and managed alike, particularly in the area of delegation.

While your company may not have in place a comparable programme, you can develop less formal techniques in your own area. They will produce the kind of atmosphere and attitudes that can make your own delegating techniques more effective.

Why participation gets results

'Work consists of whatever a body is obliged to do, and play consists of whatever a body is not obliged to do,' Mark Twain pointed out. We see this principle in action when it comes to hobbies. People spend hours 'working' in a garden, programming a home computer, tinkering in a shop, or creating intricate needlepoint. Winston Churchill even took up bricklaying as a recreation.

Why do spare-time activities bring out enthusiasm and dedication in people, when their jobs often leave them cold? As Twain notes, they're obliged to work. When they're not obliged, even the same activity becomes play.

The question is how to get your people to bring the same motivation to work-related tasks that they do to their leisure activities. Part of the answer is participation. Though you can't give your subordinates total freedom to decide, the more input they have into setting goals and devising their own methods, the more motivated they will be.

Take the case of two production teams in a factory making custom electrical-mechanical equipment for the computer industry. The supervisor of one team set a target of producing 75 components a month. His team produced 72. The manager of the other team sat down with his people and let them discuss how many components they thought they could produce. They set their own goal of 82 units and actually produced 85. The difference? Participation.

There's another angle to allowing the people who do the jobs to participate in deciding how to get them done. At a General Motors plant in Tarrytown, NY, the company's industrial engineers had used time and motion studies to determine how workers in the door trim unit were to fix the trim around the frame. The engineers knew that it took fewer motions when the worker installed the top screw first, and the rest of the screws in sequence from top to bottom.

A worker showed his foreman, however, that by installing the bottom screw second, the holes in the trim would automatically align to the holes in the door frame. The technique saved many seconds of time for each trim over the method devised by the engineers. General Motors' managers approved the change. The number of door trims installed per hour soared, spurred on not only by a better method but also by better morale resulting from workers' participation in deciding the best method. All wisdom does not reside in the minds of the bosses. There's a lot of it to be found on the shop floor.

It's also useful to give your subordinates a sense of participation in long-term decisions affecting their careers. Ask them, 'Where do you see yourself heading? What do you want to be doing two, three, five years from now? What areas of your work especially interest you? What skills would you like to develop?' In addition to giving them a feeling of participation, this kind of discussion can point to new areas for delegation.

Territory and guarding one's patch

Psychologists have found that humans share with other animals a sense of territoriality. That is, people feel comfortable and secure on their own patch. And they will vigorously protect their territory. They resent encroachment, just as animals do. You know yourself how you feel when someone uses your office without your permission when you're away. Or enters your home uninvited. You feel that your territory has been violated.

Delegation is a way of letting your subordinates stake out their own 'territories'. You tell them, 'It's your ball — run with it, handle it. Take credit for what you do.' Your subordinate takes over the task. You've given him or her space to work, to make decisions. An interesting parallel is found in Chinese agricultural communes. Somewhat to the chagrin of the central government, workers produced greater yields on the small plots given to them for their own use than they did on the larger, presumably more efficient communal fields. They took more care and produced more because the territory was their own.

The concept of territoriality argues for good delegation. Sketch out for your subordinates discrete areas of responsibility. Give them room to make decisions. Give them space. Don't crowd them or encroach on their territories by unnecessary interference. Let them enjoy the fruits of their labour in their particular areas.

Rules of thumb

The more often you delegate, the more quickly you will develop a feel for the psychology of delegation. The following rules of thumb help point you in the right direction as you pick up your own delegation instincts:

- Power through people, not power over people.
- Trust builds trust.
- Motivate, don't manipulate.
- Give them room.
- Praise in public, reproach in private.
- Achievement encourages, fear inhibits.
- Participation helps motivation.
- Communicate, don't confront.

Chapter 8

Control for Results

'Delegation without follow-through is abdication,' says Andrew Grove, president of one of Silicon Valley's blue chip companies, Intel Corporation, in his book *High Output Management.* 'You can never wash your hands of a task. Even after you delegate it, you are still responsible for its accomplishment.'

Grove has hit on an important paradox of delegation: you assign a task to a subordinate, yet you remain responsible for its completion. The paradox is resolved through controls. Controls are more than just an important aspect of delegating. These two management tools are an inseparable pair. Delegation might be compared with the wind that holds the kite in the air. But without the string − control − the kite would sail off and soon founder.

What is control?

The word control has two related meanings. The first is 'to restrain'. You control your emotions. Brakes control the speed of a car. The second meaning is 'to check or verify'. Your company's financial controller is so called because that person controls expenditures, checks and verifies the flow of money within the company.

Controls in management, and in delegation in particular, usually relate to the second meaning. By using controls, you are not trying to restrain the subordinates to whom you have delegated. Rather, you are checking their progress, verifying that they are on the right track. Keeping this in mind will prevent you from stifling subordinates through over-restrictive controls.

The purpose of controls

Controls are not bureaucratic niceties, not formalities that allow you to defend your rear. Instead, controls are a means of attaining results. Controls for their own sake are as useless as the delegation of purposeless work. They are like driving a car with one foot on the accelerator and the other on the brake.

Controls achieve results in a variety of ways. Some aid by measuring activity against a standard. For example, an operating budget compares actual spending to planned spending. A production schedule compares the actual rate of work against the planned rate. Both indicate progress towards results. Both organise and coordinate activities in order to promote efficiency. Both draw attention to deviations that will lead the organisation away from desired goals.

Other types of controls guide long-term activities. A capital budget, for example, plots major spending a year or more ahead so that the company can achieve desired expansion within its financial capabilities. A marketing plan allows for the rational introduction and promotion of new products.

Controls can give feedback that keeps activities on the path towards results. A gauge on a boiler indicates that the pressure is rising. A worker turns down the heat. The boiler returns to the desired pressure. A sales rep's weekly reports indicate to his manager that he is having trouble closing sales. The manager takes action, suggests some things the rep is doing wrong. His record begins to improve. The control, the weekly report, has led to better results — improved sales techniques.

Controls also motivate. A deadline is an example of this type of control. You have agreed with your subordinate that a report is to be finished by a certain date. As the deadline approaches, the person puts in extra effort to complete the task.

Controls, therefore, have a purpose: results. You cannot measure the effectiveness of controls unless you know the result you are aiming for. For example, a budget is a plan that aims at the maximum efficiency of an operation. If a manager sticks religiously to a budget, the control has 'worked' in a superficial sense. But by doing so, perhaps

the manager has passed up opportunities to expand production, reduce costs through higher volume, and ultimately
operate more efficiently. The control, the budget, has not in
this case led to the desired results. Think, then, about results
first. Make sure your controls lead you towards goals and
don't become goals in themselves.

Never take a casual attitude towards controls. They
shouldn't be afterthoughts or trappings. A vivid example of
how important they can be to a company can be seen in the
1984 collapse of Continental Illinois National Bank & Trust
Co. The roots of this failure, the largest in the history of
US banking, have been traced directly to weak controls.
The bank distributed hundreds of millions of dollars in highly
questionable loans without top managers really being aware
of the seriousness of the problem. Controls weren't in place.
Even the most basic controls, proper documentation of
each loan, were neglected. This lack of controls turned one
of the nation's premier banks into a house of cards. And
when the cards came tumbling down, Continental shareholders found their investment virtually wiped out.

The key to control — accountability

How can you as a manager make sure that your subordinates
in fact complete the tasks you have delegated to them and
achieve the results you've both agreed on? The answer, if it
can be stated in a word, is accountability. After delegating,
you don't just close the door of your office and stick your
head in the sand like a startled ostrich. You make sure
that your subordinates remain accountable to you, as shown
in the 'Circle of delegation' illustrated on page 132 and
further tracked in the following case study.

A sales manager uses controls

Assume you're a sales manager. You've divided your territory into 10 geographic areas and have placed a district
manager in charge of each one. Each of your district managers
supervises an average of seven sales representatives. These
managers normally report directly to you on all matters.

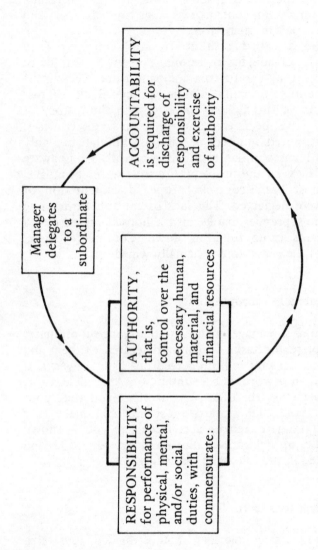

RESPONSIBILITY for performance of physical, mental, and/or social duties, with commensurate:

AUTHORITY, that is, control over the necessary human, material, and financial resources

Manager delegates to a subordinate

ACCOUNTABILITY is required for discharge of responsibility and exercise of authority

Reprinted by permission of the publisher, from *Elements of Modern Management*, by Eugene J Benge and the Editors of Alexander Hamilton Institute, p130 © 1976 AMACOM, a division of American Management Associations, New York. All rights reserved.

Circle of delegation

Your assistant sales manager, a person some years your junior, has risen to his position from the sales force. His primary duties involve overseeing your internal sales organisation.

Each month, all the district sales managers must submit to you report forms that cover the activities of each of the sales reps who work in their districts. The reports cover such things as gross cash volume by sales rep, units sold by type, number of calls made, comparisons with last year's activity, days spent in the field making calls on customers, new accounts opened, time spent on promotion activities, and many other details. As sales manager, you must submit to your company's executive committee a monthly narrative report interpreting the information gleaned from these reports.

One big time-consuming and routine chore for you is summarising this mass of data tabulated from the district manager's reports. While years of experience allow you to make these summaries with no problem, you believe you could spend this time on less routine and more productive duties such as planning sales strategy. Furthermore, some of the district managers have fallen into the annoying habit of submitting their reports late. These delays put pressure on you in meeting your own deadline for your monthly report to the executive committee.

Your assistant currently manages and administers the internal office sales staff — the order clerks, sales correspondents, and clerical help — and also backstops for you when you travel. You decide to delegate to your assistant the jobs of summarising the reports from the district managers and making sure those managers submit their reports on time. You think that this will not only relieve you of a routine chore, but will also develop your assistant's skills and prepare him to take over your job or a similar position elsewhere in the company.

Here are the steps you go through as you pass on the task in the manner outlined by the 'Circle of delegation':

1. You call in your assistant and get his agreement on the results to be achieved: the tabulation of the sales reps' data into a coherent and useful report plus stepped-up compliance by the reps on their reporting deadline. You talk

with him about how the delegated task will provide an opportunity for him to develop some new skills and will enlarge and enrich his position. Both of you agree on the amount of authority he will need to go with the new responsibility.

2. You notify the district managers that your assistant will now be handling these new tasks. You emphasise the importance of the report that you make to the executive committee and how it can have some impact on the committee's decisions in such areas as compensation, advertising, and promotion expenditures.

3. You let the district managers know that your assistant has the authority to ask for and receive their reports directly.

4. You also let the managers know that from now on their reports must be submitted at the same time as their monthly expense accounts and that your assistant has the authority to hold up any expense reimbursement until the report is received.

5. You set a deadline for the manager to have the summary in your hands by the fifteenth of each month. You also advise him or her to let you know when any district manager has failed to submit a report by the tenth of the month.

6. You get your subordinate's agreement that his future performance will be judged, in part, by how well he accomplishes these newly delegated duties.

7. Finally, you emphasize to your assistant that he is entirely accountable to you for the results you've both agreed upon.

You've now completed the loop in the 'Circle of delegation'. You've given your assistant the tools to get the delegated duties done — the responsibility and just the right amount of authority. You've given him power and provided an incentive to the district managers to follow your assistant's directions. You've put in a control, or a standard, for him to meet through reporting exceptions — that is, to let you know which managers don't report on time. You've retained ultimate control over your assistant through his accountability to you. That accountability is the key to the delegation process. It ensures that you get the results you want from the new duty you've delegated.

Control systems

The case just given is a true one. It's a system that the sales manager of an actual company used to control the task that he delegated. While the case makes a neat package explaining how to control a delegated duty, it doesn't cover all the control methods that you should know about and can use in your own delegations.

Other techniques and systems may better fit your own organisation. They may suit your own style of managing better, or the style you select in a particular situation. Other systems may make a better fit with the psychology of the delegatees you have available. These other control systems let you choose other ways to delegate the tasks you are assigning to your subordinates.

Setting control standards

Any system, method, or technique of control for delegated tasks should first be made up of standards of performance. When you set standards to develop the control plan, you should use the same standards to measure results achieved from executing the plan. If, for instance, your plan calls for your delegatee to process 20 orders a day, then your measurement should also be 20 orders a day.

In the above example, you saw that the sales manager had set at least two control standards for his assistant: (1) his assistant must notify him if any district manager has not submitted his report by the tenth of the month; and (2) his assistant must submit a summary to the manager by the fifteenth of the month.

However, standards by themselves do not control. They are merely goals against which performance should be compared. Objectives, policies, guidelines, rules, procedures, and organisational structures can be used as standards. But they do not control by themselves.

A stunning example of how guidelines are actually passive and how they are not in themselves control mechanisms surfaced as a result of *TV Guide's* story about a CBS documentary *The Uncounted Enemy — A Vietnam Depression*. In an interview reported in *New York* magazine (23 January,

1984), the president of CBS News stated that CBS staff are given a copy of 64 guidelines for preparation of documentaries. They are required to sign a statement that they have received and read the guidelines. Yet, CBS's own internal enquiry into the *TV Guide* allegations of misuse of the guidelines did not refute the allegations — though the enquiry did support CBS's contention that the broadcast was fair and impartial. In short, the guidelines did not control the actions of the persons who prepared this documentary. You'll see more clearly why standards alone cannot control delegated responsibilities when you consider how they are arrived at and what purposes they serve in control of delegated tasks.

Understanding control standards

Before you delve into the specifics of control functions, you should understand more about standards and how they are used, particularly in connection with duties you've delegated. A standard is some measure that has been fixed, either arbitrarily by one person or by general consent. Standards are usually expressed in terms of quality, quantity, cost, or time.

A sales manager may decide that three-piece suits of muted colours, white shirts, and regimental ties are the 'uniforms' that the sales reps should wear when calling on customers or prospects. That's an arbitrary standard against which the attire of all sales reps will be measured. Or an industrial engineer will decide after study that a worker can install 10 door trim units an hour — another arbitrary standard, at least in a non-union shop.

On the other hand, as illustrated at Volvo's assembly plant in Kalmo, Sweden, groups of workers who have appropriate skills assemble Volvos in separate bays or work areas. They are provided with all materials, access to tools, and other support necessary to complete the assembly of an entire automobile. The groups operate at their own speeds, and the output of each bay — the number of cars built in any period of time — is the result of the general consent of all members of the group. What the group agrees on becomes the standard for its own production bay.

You can set standards only for limited periods of time.

In continuous production operations they remain in place longer than in job shops, in offices, or in management of professional personnel. It's often impractical to stop a production run abruptly because some better procedure has been developed. When you do change a standard, you set a different level of output. You can't assume that any standard is permanent.

What you measure is what you get

After accountability, the choice of the right control standard is the essence of formulating effective controls. Management expert Peter Drucker puts it succinctly: 'The basic question is not "How do we control?" but "What do we measure in our control system?" '

Control standards always look towards results. In the above example, the sales manager was above all interested in timeliness. He wanted the district managers' reports submitted to his assistant on time, and the assistant's compilation of the data handed to him promptly. His controls — deadlines of the tenth and fifteenth of each month — therefore focus on punctual completion of the task and subtasks.

Or consider the example of the customer complaint manager of a department store chain. As business expanded she was assigned two assistants. She delegated to them the task of handling routine complaints. As a control standard, she determined that each assistant should record and pass on to the appropriate department at least 30 complaints each day. A problem developed immediately. The assistants, endeavouring to meet the standard, became abrupt with customers and passed on complaints without seriously considering the best way they could be resolved. The manager realised that this was her own fault. She'd chosen an inappropriate measure or standard. To rectify the situation, she selected a new standard: that each assistant should successfully resolve at least 20 complaints a day. This standard directed the assistants' efforts towards the true goal of the delegation — to resolve complaints to the customer's satisfaction — and didn't push them to simply go through the motions for the sake of handling a set number of complaints.

This is an illustration of the principle 'What you measure is what you get'. Standards influence behaviour. The production foreman whose standard is 100 pieces an hour will try to push work forward at any cost. The foreman whose standard is 90 *good* pieces an hour will pay as much attention to quality as to quantity. The sales rep who is compensated purely on volume will try to sell as much as possible to any customer. The sales rep whose standards include profitability of accounts will pay more attention to product mix, customer creditworthiness, and other factors affecting earnings.

When setting standards, always try to look at quality as well as quantity. Easily quantifiable aspects of a task may provide the most convenient standards, but ask yourself if they will lead to the results you're after. Keep in mind, too, that each individual standard focuses on a narrow phase of a task. A thermostat measures heat, but not humidity. An operating budget measures expenditures, but not customer satisfaction. Try to achieve a balance. If you've delegated to the supervisors under you the task of getting their people to take a training course, don't use as a standard simply the number of employees taking the course, but include as well some measure of the improvement in skills that results.

One last point is to make sure your control standard is in fact controllable by the delegatee. If the sales manager in the above example had set as a standard the accuracy of the data submitted in the district managers' reports, he would have been holding his assistant accountable for a factor over which he really had no control. In the same way, you can't apply to a maintenance manager the standard of a set level of fuel expenditures in a period of rapidly rising fuel prices. His control over expenditures is quite limited and the standard serves no purpose.

Limitations of control standards

Standards have limitations as controls. As mentioned before, setting standards for delegatees doesn't mean that what you want done will get done or that you'll get the results you're aiming at. Standards are no more than mechanisms that *should* trigger a response.

Life for delegators would be easier if they could develop

automatic responses, such as those that are possible with mechanical or electrical sensors, numerically controlled machines, or programmed computers. But managers delegate to people, an entirely different ball game. And, as you'll see, automatic controls aren't perfect. Suppose you could automate your control of subordinates through a system similar to thermostatic control of room temperature. Would that be a satisfactory control?

Let's first review how that kind of automatic control works before deciding to turn poeple into 'thermostats'. When the temperature of a room falls below a certain level, a thermostat makes an electrical connection that turns on some heating element, such as a gas burner, to get the temperature back up to standard. But thermostats don't come close to giving perfect control. They can't, for instance, anticipate a fall in temperature. They react to it. What triggered the electrical connection in the first place was an error — the temperature fell below standard. And at the other end the thermostat controls by another error — the room gets too hot, the thermostat breaks the electrical connection, and the heater goes off.

Controlling before failure occurs

What parallels do automatic controls have to controls for delegated tasks, duties, and jobs? Standards for the results expected from the delegation should be set, just as someone sets the standard for the temperature of a room to be automatically controlled by a thermostat. But managers or delegators who want to control need not and in fact must not wait for errors or failures to occur before they begin their follow-through.

The illustration given previously of the sales manager lacks one very important aspect: the standard that he set, to be informed within ten days if a district manager failed to send in his report, means that a failure has occurred. Likewise, his standard for his assistant to have the summary in his hands by the fifteenth of the month also means that if the summary arrives late, his assistant has failed. Both instances force the sales manager into action to correct failure *after* it has taken place.

How can delegation controls overcome this problem? Only by controlling the operations before the failures occur — by using preventive measures to lessen the need for corrective, possibly emergency, actions. These preventive measures, which range from rules and policies to coaching and direct supervisions, will be covered in the next chapter.

Managerial control and delegation control

In a real sense there are few substantive differences between controls related to delegated duties or tasks and other managerial controls. Management control occurs when systems are planned and set up so that all parts of the company adjust to changes, both internal and external. Some management 'experts' spend so much time trying to develop automatic controls that work as well as thermostats, they can't see that all such controls wait for and depend on failures before they are activated to remedy the situation. Better to search out ways to anticipate trouble.

For example, suppose your company suddenly loses a large customer. An automatic system should begin a chain reaction that ripples through the whole organisation. The purchasing agents should reduce their orders to hold down inventories. The production manager should slow production. Personnel should reduce staffing. Unfortunately, however, these automatic actions are too late to prevent delivery of supplies on order, increased inventories, and over-production. You need only read your daily newspaper to find examples of companies in crisis because they relied too heavily on automatic control systems — thermostats, if you will — that didn't take effect until failures had occurred.

A classic example of just this sort of thing happened at W T Grant & Co. Among the numerous management mistakes that caused the bankruptcy of this once major retailer was a cash flow crisis causes in part by buyers overstocking goods long after the warning signals were flying that these were not the products that Grant's customer wanted.

The need for controls that anticipate

This brief discussion of managerial controls shows that

managers need flexible, anticipatory controls as well as automatic controls for successful delegation. Delegators must continually monitor and evaluate all conditions that may affect the tasks, duties, and jobs they have delegated. Remember, delegation without follow-through is abdication. Once you, as a delegator, have abdicated responsibility for a delegated task, you have thrown open the door for a breakdown of the whole system.

Return again to the case of the sales manager's monthly report to his executive committee. The committee has delegated responsibility for sales to the manager, but remains a controller by comparing reported sales to planned levels. When sales don't meet projections, planned anticipatory flexibility makes it easy to shift to new sales forecasts and new standards. These controls buy time to develop new promotions and new products, or to alter customer perceptions of current company products.

It's true that evidence of failure — falling below the sales goal — triggers a change in plans and standards. But when you combine feedback, or thermostat kind of controls, with preliminary contingency planning for deviations, and the tracking of trouble spots to anticipate changes, you eliminate or reduce actions that aim at nothing more than 'putting out the fires'.

Selecting a control system

Selecting the right control system for a delegated task requires careful observation of the situation. In general, most systems can be classified as either mechanistic or dynamic.

Mechanistic systems

Examples include rules, quotas, deadlines, and criteria. Mechanistic systems are best for short-term assignments or long-term duties in a stable environment. These controls function by punishing mistakes. They involve frequent checks of the process as much as looks at the overall results. They tend to be specific and imposed from outside. Their goal is efficiency.

141

Dynamic systems

Examples include job descriptions, performance appraisals, and strategic plans. Dynamic systems work best for long-term assignments or any assignments in an unstable atmosphere. They function more by rewarding success than by punishing mistakes. Checks are infrequent. Results, not methods, are the focus. They lay out general goals, usually with input from the person being controlled.

These two types of control system can be compared with the stick and the carrot. One discourages deviation, the other encourages achievement. In most situations, a combination of controls is called for. A subordinate may be spurred to do well on a delegated assignment because that person is looking for praise from a forthcoming performance appraisal. But a separate control system, a specific deadline, may be what actually assures that the person completes the task on time.

Chapter 9

Effective Control Techniques

To get the best results from delegation, you need techniques that give control before, during, and after the task that you're delegating takes place. That means combining usable automatic controls (the equivalent of a thermostat, a closed sequence system) with functions that are called 'open sequence'. Open sequence systems anticipate and set actions in motion before errors or failure occur. To use the temperature analogy again, if a sudden weather change drops the outside temperature rapidly, an open sequence turns the heater on *before* the inside room temperature falls below the desired level. No failure occurs.

Preactivity controls or the preventive defence

Preactivity controls aim to prevent delegatees from making mistakes. They include policy and procedures, routine planning, scheduling, preparation, and despatching. All are aimed at pointing the delegatee in the right direction from the beginning.

Policy and procedures

These are the bedrock of control in delegation. They provide a body of assumptions that save you, as a manager, from having to spell out in long detail the ways that a subordinate should react to the contingencies surrounding every delegated task. For example, when you delegate to your assistant the task of visiting district offices, you don't have to make clear to that person not to take his or her spouse along at company expense. Standing policy controls the person's behaviour in the situation. Nor do you have to emphasise that a subordinate to whom you are delegating customer contact is to treat all customers with courtesy and respect. Company policy so dictates. If delegates use their own cars on assignments, they needn't come to you to ask about reimbursement. Instead, they simply follow a set procedure. Policy and procedures therefore guide — that is, control — the efforts of your subordinates.

In the early 1960s, when Xerox Corporation was one of the United States' fastest growing companies, then president Joseph Wilson made a very astute decision. During the hectic period of fast growth, most contingencies had been decided through personal feedback. A subordinate asked his manager how to proceed in a given situation. Maybe the manager had to ask his or her boss. The decision was made ad hoc. Wilson saw that such a system would mean management chaos as the company grew ever larger. He instituted a formal body of policies and procedures that covered a wide range of contingencies. Arguments that these rules made the company too rigid soon faded as managers realised that they also made life a lot easier and helped to coordinate efforts and prevent wasted time. The policies helped to change Xerox from an 'adolescent' into a mature and established company.

Policy refers to general guidelines. Procedures cover behaviour in specific situations. For example, policy dictates that a company's products be of high quality. Procedures tell quality control inspectors how to go about sampling and testing production runs. Policy states the need for management development. Procedures prescribe the timing and content of training programmes.

Make sure, in delegating tasks to subordinates, that you review the policies and procedures that apply. They can aid you by serving as effective fundamental controls. But they can also hinder you if you are too casual about them. For example, if you delegate a task that requires your subordinate to tap the resources of another department, but ignore the policy that requires you to receive the permission of the manager of that department in advance, then your subordinate will encounter problems that will return to plague you.

Routine planning

Before you can actually delegate a task, you need to give out information and get together the orders for action that you're going to give. As discussed in the last chapter, in delegating the report summarisation the sales manager first called in his assistant to discuss the delegation and to secure agreement on how it should be accomplished. He also planned in a preliminary way how to let his district managers know that they should send their reports to his assistant rather than to himself. He gathered or marshalled the directions he would give. In planning, the sales manager anticipated that his assistant could fail on some points. His plans were part of his 'preventive defence' against possible failures.

Scheduling

The sales manager then notified his assistant and his district managers of the timing of the changes. He emphasised, through the tie-in of expense account reimbursement, the importance of their getting the reports to the assistant on time. He let them know that the assistant's summary, from which he developed his interpretation for the executive committee, would have a bearing on the committee's decisions on compensation, advertising, and promotion expenditures. Furthermore, he set deadlines for submission of their reports and also made sure they knew when his report was due. As with routine planning, this delegation control method is designed to stop errors before they can happen. Scheduling makes sure that all the activities surrounding a delegated task mesh, and prevents the disruptive grinding of gears that occurs when they don't.

Preparation

The next step in this preactivity control of the newly delegated task was to let the district managers know that the assistant now had the responsibility and authority to carry out the delegation. As another part of the preparation, the sales manager developed the format of the assistant's summary of the reports so that it would give the information in the way he wanted it. It was his 'preventive defence' against the assistant's botching the job of summarising. Also, he had to prepare forms to combine activity reports with expense reimbursement, and see that they were printed and sent to the district managers. This control anticipated the possibility that managers would make the mistake of sending in reports and expense accounts separately. Preparation, in general, controls because it establishes a 'groove' for the delegatee to work in; it gets the person started on the right foot.

Despatching

This term, as used in delegation, generally means releasing to delegatees authority to act in increments, a little at a time. When the sales manager linked the district managers' activity reports to reimbursement of their expenses and instructed the assistant to reimburse only when the reports arrived on time with the expense account, he released to his assistant some, but not all, of his authority over the district managers.

You should bear in mind when you work out your own system of despatching authority that subordinates often overreact to newly given power. The control that the sales manager gave was to withhold expense reimbursement *only* when accounts were *not* accompanied by activity reports. He did not give the assistant authority to demand activity reports prior to their deadline or unconnected with expense accounts. He controlled the potential for his assistant to overreact.

Assessing preactivity controls

Preactivity controls are all aimed at prevention — at anticipating and avoiding mistakes that a delegatee might make and guiding him or her through contingencies. But while this preventive approach represents a strength, it can also turn into a weakness. All contingencies can never be foreseen. Policies and procedures will not guide the delegatee in every situation. Rather than adequately controlling subordinates' activities, planning, scheduling, and preparation may lock them into inappropriate reactions.

For example, what if the assistant sales manager begins to receive reports from a district manager that contain

146

discrepancies? Sales don't match customer calls, for example. None of the preactivity controls has foreseen this contingency, so none of them really controls the assistant in this situation. In fact, if his preparation has given him the idea that as long as the data in a report is complete it should be incorporated with his tabulation, then the preactivity control may actually steer him away from taking the initiative and pointing out the discrepancies to his boss.

Clearly, you cannot stop at preactivity controls. You cannot feel that, having set the delegatee in the right direction, you can just sit back and wait for the person to reach the destination. Control must continue. The next level of controls are those that guide the delegatee while the task is being carried out, real-time controls.

Real-time controls

These kinds of control affect the delegated work while it is going on. They are 'on line' with the activity, rather than occurring before or after. Still, they are part of the preventive system that keeps failures at a minimum. They place a premium on people as controllers rather than on events that act as automatic triggers. They anticipate as well as correct. The sales manager anticipated that district managers might forget to send reports and expense accounts together, so he combined the forms.

Real-time controls really begin with despatching. Despatching straddles the predelegation controls and the controls that govern both during and after the delegated work takes place. Despatching is like a three-legged stool. It has a leg in each camp of before, during, and after. The deadlines given to the district managers for their reports, and to the assistant for his summaries, were controls designed to prevent delays before the tasks were delegated. They continued to control the timely submission of the reports after the duties began. Among the functions that real-time controls include, beyond despatching of authority, are directing, supervising, correcting, and coaching.

Directing

This is another way of describing communication. Directing

147

by word of mouth generally works best. Usually a superior delegates to a subordinate, as in the example of the sales manager delegating to his assistant. The sales manager called his assistant into his office to discuss face-to-face the new duties he intended to delegate to him. He gave his subordinate information and understanding.

Normally, you should think of directing as an interpreting function, not necessarily one of commanding, as the word 'direct' sometimes implies. General Electric, long known for its excellence in developing managers, has established the Management Development Institute at Croton-on-Hudson, New York. The Institute's programmes have been recognised as the equals of most university programmes devoted to the same purposes. As a corollary to developing managers, the Institute's staff came up with a definition of managing. General Electric includes 'directing' as one of the skills that make up the art of management. Its definition says that managing is the art of getting things done through people by means of persuasion rather than by command. But the definition includes a footnote that states that when persuasion fails, managers should resort to command. Directing, then, while usually an interpreting function, can include commanding when necessary.

Directing begins at the same time as the delegated activity. For instance, when you assign a task to your administrative assistant, you begin to direct when that person begins the task. Suppose you delegate the job of answering certain kinds of letters. You begin to give directions as soon as your assistant begins responding to such letters. Naturally, any delegatee will make many small decisions without needing direction. But directing is a control that responds, when the need arises, to contingencies. It prevents the person from making a series of decisions that carries the course of action away from the intended result.

Supervising

We need to emphasise that delegating without follow-up is just sloughing off something you don't want to do, getting rid of an unwanted chore. Some managers are so cavalier about shedding responsibilities that they don't even bother to keep their fingers crossed to help their subordinates get their jobs done.

Supervising makes sure that subordinates are, in fact, following the directions, plans, and instructions that you've given them. You can't expect that you'll always get the results you want through supervising. But it is one of the controls you use to help you towards those results. Supervising means watching. It is a kind of looking over the shoulders of delegatees without meddling or breathing down their necks. You can be sure that the sales manager reviewed his assistant's first summary even while he was preparing it.

Supervising helps you catch things when they're drifting away from plans. It helps you to get your delegatees back on course before damage is done. Interestingly, managers can delegate routine supervision to other subordinates. The supervising as a control function does not need to be done by the delegators themselves. For instance, a plant superintendent can delegate a task to a foreman, but have another foreman do the supervision. Of course, that doesn't free the plant superintendent from his responsibility for results.

Corrections

Correction goes along with supervision. It simply means that, once you spot something that the delegatee is doing wrong, or some obstacle over which the person has no control, you take action. This may mean bringing the delegatee's activity back in line with the original plan. Or it may mean altering the plan to accommodate the contingency. Or, finally, it may mean changing both the activity and the plan to bring them together. For example, you delegate to a subordinate the task of conducting a survey of customer attitudes. This person finds that the form for recording the responses, which you've developed together, leaves out many categories of answers. The subordinate begins writing in customers' replies. In the process of supervision, you note this activity. But because it will make computerisation of the forms more difficult, you take corrective action. You change the activity, requesting the subordinate to cease writing in replies, and you also change the plan: you help the person design a new, more comprehensive form for recording responses.

Usually corrections mean bringing the subordinate's activity back in line with the plan. If you've done well in mapping out your preliminary controls of planning, scheduling, preparing, and despatching, you should seldom need to make changes in standards of performance. But also remember that plans are guides towards goals, not goals in themselves. Adapt to the circumstances as you find them. Don't be afraid to change course when necessary.

Coaching

Directing has to do with relaying information and instructions to the delegatee. Supervision involves seeing that those instructions are carried out. Correcting means rectifying errors and altering direction. Coaching is the fourth, and equally important, real-time control. Essentially, coaching is a daily, informal flow of questions, suggestions, constructive criticism, and praise between you and your subordinates.

For example, the chief of engineering stops by the work area of a young design engineer to whom he's delegated a tricky specification problem. Perhaps he says nothing and moves on. Maybe he asks, 'How's it going?' in order to give the engineer a chance to ask a question or raise a problem. Perhaps he corrects an incipient mistake that the engineer hasn't spotted yet. Maybe he only offers a few words of encouragement. All of these possibilities are open in coaching. All of them ensure that the delegated task proceeds towards the desired results, thus serving as controls.

Coaching in delegation resembles coaching in sports. The coach is there when needed. He points out mistakes that the players can't see themselves. He suggests trying out different techniques, but he doesn't impose ways of bowling not suited to an individual. He gives the benefit of his experience.

Coaching requires, above all, openness; a spirit of collaboration, not of confrontation. If a batsman feigns an injury, or hides real problems, effective coaching becomes impossible. If subordinates feel that they can't be open with their bosses out of fear of a reprimand, then little communication will occur.

Coaching also requires you to listen. If directing and correcting involve talking, and supervising means watching, then coaching requires, above all, listening. To be an effective control, it demands two-way communication. Try to empathise with subordinates. As you listen, put yourself in their shoes. Maybe the delegated task would be a stroll through the park for you. But for an inexperienced subordinate it may seem as tough as climbing Mount Everest. Don't assume you know what problems delegatees will run into, or what advice they will need. Listen.

While coaching should be informal, it need not be completely spontaneous. Since it's best to communicate with the delegatee at his or her work area, make a point of casually calling on all your subordinates daily. Don't waste time just chatting, but let them know that you are available for coaching. When discussing problems, don't trail off into generalities. Stick to the specific instance at hand. Be concise without being abrupt. Make sure, too, that you shape your coaching to the individual. With whom are you talking? What are that person's individual needs? Moral support? Technical advice? A reining in of excess zeal? A nudge to speed up the work?

Coaching has, in innumerable situations, proved to be one of the best real-time control techniques. It prevents problems, provides motivation, and helps subordinates to develop skills in on-the-job situations. It also takes time. Coaching won't work as a control if you only get around to it once a month. But where do you gain the time to coach? You delegate. Just as coaching will make your delegation more effective, so delegating your time-consuming tasks and routine work will give you the time to coach.

Assessing real-time controls

Preactivity controls have the disadvantage of not enabling you to foresee all contingencies. Real-time controls specifically deal with contingencies. Therefore, they serve to keep the delegatee on track. They prevent small problems from growing into major disruptions. They continually direct the person's efforts towards desired goals.

But the disadvantage that you can easily encounter with real-time controls is that they tend towards over-control. They make you want to get in on the action. Too much directing can cut into subordinates' decision making. Too much supervision and correcting can undercut their initiative.

Coaching can encourage subordinates to become dependent on you, to expect you to solve all their problems. The line between controls that guide and controls that stifle can be a very fine one. Effective real-time controls that don't over-control are part of the art of delegating that you will develop with experience.

Post-activity controls

No delegated task exists in a vacuum. You rarely delegate to a subordinate only once. Usually, by the time the person finishes a task, you've passed on one or more additional delegations. For this reason, post-activity controls are important. Obviously, they can't influence the outcome of the activity they're concerned with. They can, however, prevent mistakes from recurring. They can also contribute to subordinates' motivation by providing rewards for a job well done and by pointing out ways in which the person can improve his or her performance in the future.

The evaluation session

Not all delegated tasks require the follow-up of an evaluation session, a discussion with the subordinate of the outcome of the delegation. For significant tasks, though, such a session provides a number of advantages. First, it gives you an opportunity to let delegatees know how they've performed. Even when the success of a project seems obvious to you, the subordinate will still profit from your specific words of approval and commendation. This is especially the case when the person has encountered numerous difficulties along the way. Delegatees may become so wrapped up in the delays, frustrations, and obstacles surrounding the task that they lose sight of the fact that everything turned out successfully in the end, that they accomplished the goals they went after.

An evaluation session also gives you an opportunity to encourage delegatees to learn from their mistakes. In a chess game a player may make an error. He knows something has gone wrong because he sees the tide of the game turn against him. But it is only after the game is over, when he goes back to analyse it, that the true significance of the mistake — its effect on the game and the ways it could have been prevented or its consequences limited — become clear.

For example, as production manager, you've delegated to an assistant the task of designing an assembly procedure for a new component. In the middle of the project, you discover that she is creating a bottleneck in an attempt to make the delivery of parts more efficient. You point out the problem and suggest a different direction. But only when the entire project is complete, and she has an opportunity to view her original mistake in the light of the whole procedure, can she fully grasp where she would have gone wrong.

A third benefit of evaluation sessions following a delegation is to review the original goals and control standards in the light of the finished task. For example, if the sales manager in the case we've been discussing sits down with his assistant after three months, perhaps together they will determine that the tabulation of the data should be handed to the manager on the twelfth of the month, not the fifteenth. The previous standard had not allowed enough time for the manager to prepare his report to the executive committee. A new standard was called for.

The performance appraisal

This is another post-activity control. It concerns not just a single delegated task, but a series of delegations over a period of time. Naturally, it also goes into subordinates' performance on their primary duties. By including a discussion of delegation in a performance appraisal, managers can help subordinates appreciate the role of delegation in teaching new skills. They can expand subordinates' understanding of the scope of the company and their position in it.

Performance appraisals offer an excellent oppportunity for you to conduct a general discussion of delegation. Often, in the rush to get work done, you skip over such things as the reasons for delegating, the assumptions and expectations that go along with delegated tasks, the need for subordinates' participation in goal setting, and the reasons for control systems. Likewise, you can take up any general questions that the subordinate has about the delegation process. Some of the issues relating to delegation that you might want to cover are:

- Whether the subordinate feels that he or she is receiving enough delegated tasks, or too many
- How the person fits delegated tasks into his or her schedule of routine duties
- New areas in which the person would like to receive delegated responsibilities
- Any general problems with authority, resources, or human relations that have been affecting the person's performance on delegated tasks
- The specific role of delegation in your evaluation of the person's performance and decisions about his or her promotion
- Forthcoming tasks that you intend to delegate to the person and which he or she could begin to prepare for.

Reward and punishment

Rewards and punishments are motivational controls. They do not in themselves correct errors or guide behaviour. Rather, they encourage delegatees to make their own sustained efforts towards goals. You already know that a manager has to recognise and reward success in delegated tasks. Often, recognition itself is an adequate reward. Make sure that delegatees know that you know when they've done a good job. Emphasise the importance of their efforts in the company's success. If you can provide something beyond a pat on the back — a bonus, pay rise, privilege, or public recognnition — you should do so as appropriate. Remember, though, to be consistent in rewards and not to promise more than you can deliver.

Punishment should be used sparingly as a control. Generally, you need only resort to penalties when a delegatee either breaks company policy in some flagrant way, or fails to make an honest effort to complete a task successfully. For example, if a subordinate deliberately goes way over the spending limit for a project, then some penalty — ranging from a reprimand to dismissal — is called for to discourage such action in the future. Again, be consistent and make sure that you yourself follow company policy to the letter.

On the other hand, delegatees who botch projects because of unforeseen problems or outside circumstances, or because you've given them duties that are beyond their current abilities, should not be penalised beyond the aggravation of the assignment itself. Instead, make every effort to identify the root of the problem and to help them pick up the pieces, learn a lesson, and do better next time. Applying penalties does nothing but make the person shy away from future delegated tasks or approach them with excess caution.

Assessing post-activity controls

The most obvious argument against post-activity controls is that they involve closing the stable door when the horse is already miles away. Clearly, these controls can never substitute for pre-activity or real-time controls. But they should not, for this reason, be neglected. A mistake on a delegated task usually has limited consequences, especially if other controls help you to catch it in time. But the lesson thoroughly learned during an evaluation session or performance appraisal can provide benefits that are unlimited. They will be immensely rewarding to the subordinate in future tasks, and in fact throughout his or her career.

Management by exception

The exception principle is one of the fundamental axioms of management. It means that only significant deviations from plan or from expected results should be called to the attention of managers. Take our example of the sales manager. He delegated to his assistant the job of summarising all the district managers' reports and empowered him to withhold reimbursement of those expense accounts not accompanied by a report. Perhaps most of the district managers' reports come in by the seventh of the month, some more on the eighth, and a few on the ninth. The assistant doesn't report these variations to his boss. Only when all the reports are not in by the tenth does an exception to standard occur. Only then does he need to act.

To make the exception principle control when delegating, you need to set up objectives, plans, and standards that leave delegatees latitude to make decisions on small variances and deviations. If they can't handle minor changes, every

155

deviation would be an exception and the exception principle wouldn't serve as an effective control.

Setting the deviation point for reporting, therefore, is the key to making management by exception work. Wide latitude means that you will rarely be bothered by reports of deviations. But it also means that once you have been notified, the problem will probably already be severe. Narrow latitude means that you will frequently receive reports, but that you will know about problems before they become critical. In this sense, a thermostat operates by exceptions. The thermostat does not 'take action' as a result of a small temperature fluctuation. If it did, it would be constantly turning the furnace off and on, resulting in an inefficient use of energy. However, if its latitude of deviation is set too broadly, the occupants of the building will find themselves first shivering, then sweating, as the temperature swings up and down. Setting the deviation point, the point of exception, establishes a balance between efficiency and comfort.

Successful management by exception pays close attention to the relative importance of the factor being measured. You may tell a subordinate to whom you've delegated a multimillion-pound project to report to you if a single expenditure exceeds projections by more than £10,000. You would hardly give the same latitude to a subordinate you put in charge of purchasing office supplies. This is comparable with the difference between the thermostat for a warehouse and that for a fur storage vault. A thermostat with very narrow 'exceptions' might be required to keep the furs at a precise temperature. But the one in the warehouse might only kick the heat in when the temperature falls below freezing.

The advantages of management by exception in delegation are several:

1. It focuses your attention on major rather than minor factors. In this way, it greatly reduces distractions and lets you focus your efforts where they will do the most good.

2. It keeps you from wasting your time reviewing delegated tasks that are running smoothly. You know you'll be notified if something goes wrong; thus, for the time being, you can forget about them.

3. It encourages your subordinates' self-direction by giving them the latitude to handle deviations within the reporting limits. It also discourages them from bringing to you trivial decisions that they should be making themselves.

4. It directs both your and your subordinates' attention towards results. What management by exception says is, 'I don't care how you get it done, as long as you accomplish the results we agreed on within the budget and before the deadline.' This turns your subordinates' effort towards goals and away from just looking good.

The exception principle, though, is no panacea. For example, the sales manager has his assistant report to him if any district manager does not file data by the tenth. But what if, on the tenth, the assistant comes in and says that he's heard from none of the district managers? The assistant has dutifully waited until the exception occurred before reporting. But now the sales manager faces the formidable task of contacting all the district managers at once and trying to pull the figures together in time. Even when using management by exception, a certain amount of supervisions, correcting, and coaching are called for.

The costs and benefits of controls

Controls cost. To begin with, they use up your time and your subordinates' time. They may also require paperwork, memos, letters, long-distance communication, or meetings. All represent costs. In addition, controls can dampen subordinates' morale and reduce their initiative — another cost.

The question you should always ask yourself is, 'Are the costs of the controls I've imposed justified by the resulting benefits?' If a simple reporting system can prevent a multi-million-pound error, obviously the benefits justify the cost. But if detailed and expensive testing results in a negligible increase in product quality, then the cost of the controls probably outweighs the benefits. Your goal is to balance costs and benefits so that your company receives the maximum overall benefit.

This balancing act requires common sense. For example, a company manufacturing expensive hand tools wanted to hold down pilfering of products. The security manager established monthly inventory counts and periodic inspection of employees' lockers. Both measures cost time and money. The firm benefited, though, to the extent that thefts shrank from an average of £4,000-worth of products a month to £600-worth. Still not satisfied, the manager considered introducing weekly inventory counts and a search of every employee leaving the premises. He estimated that this would reduce thefts to less than £300-worth of goods a month. But the much greater cost of this programme, in terms of both expense and worker morale, failed to justify the minimal benefit. The plan was discarded.

Always try to peg your level of control at a point where the resulting benefits justify the cost. The first step in doing this is to pinpoint the cost and benefits, both of which may be hidden. How much time and effort will the controls require? What mistakes and potential expense and trouble will they help to prevent? What is the chance of errors and oversights occurring? What wider ramifications would failure have on the company?

The problem of over-control

Controls are necessary and useful in all delegations. But remember that you can always have too much of a good thing. Don't try to eliminate all possible risk from delegation. The cost of such an attempt, as mentioned above, will almost always outweigh the resulting benefit. This is true because over-control in delegation always incurs the cost of stifled initiative. You may be tempted in this direction because you feel more comfortable when 'everything's under control'. But consider the following facts:

- Over-control does not return benefits comparable to its costs. Always keep in mind that your time and the degree of distraction required by a control system are costs.
- Over-control diminishes some of the essential benefits of the delegation process, namely the encouragement of initiative, independence, and decision making in your subordinates.

- Over-control often promotes the very thing it seeks to prevent. For example, if a subordinate knows that you are going to check over every figure of a statistical report, the preparation of which you've delegated, then that person is likely to become careless about making errors, knowing they will be corrected.

Where do prudent controls leave off and over-control begin? That question must be answered in the light of every individual delegation. Controls protect you and your subordinate from disaster. Over-control smothers your subordinate and imposes on you a burden of distraction and petty annoyances. Controls give both of you confidence and room to operate. Over-control seems to crowd you both. Control makes delegation successful. Over-control pulls the rug from under it.

Internal controls

When we talk of controls, we are referring to external controls: reports, instructions, questions, and directions passed between you and your delegatees. But these controls should have the further aim of promoting internal controls. Your setting goals, giving instructions, passing on information, and other forms of preparation should encourage subordinates to establish their own goals, to obtain needed information, and to prepare in advance. Your checking of subordinates' work in progress, coaching, and supervision should all aim at having them closely monitor their own work, look for errors themselves, and find their own solutions to problems. And finally, your method of reviewing and evaluating delegations should encourage them always to learn from their mistakes, to find general principles in specific situations.

The development of internal controls is important in both the long and short term. On the one hand, it takes part of the control burden off you in future delegated tasks as subordinates come to examine their own work more closely and develop a better sense of how to proceed with projects in a judicious manner. In the long run, it prepares them for leadership. Some day, one of your subordinates may be sitting in the chair you now occupy. By then, that person will need to have gained enough experience in internal

159

controls so that he or she will be beyond leaning on external controls, will be able to operate autonomously. The person's ability to do so will be a reflection of your expertise in management development.

Chapter 10

The Delegation Habit

You've acquired the delegation habit. You're delegating. You're getting rid of your routine and trivial tasks by passing them on to your subordinates. You're making more time for the real business of managing by shifting time-consuming chores to your people. Almost automatically, you choose the right person, prepare, and pass along the duty in a way that keeps everyone working towards results. You have your moments of anxiety, but the controls that you always impose are sufficient to steer your delegatees away from the treacherous shoals of costly errors without reefing their sails. Becoming a delegator hasn't been easy. But now you're reaping the rewards of delegation: getting results that you once thought were beyond your reach, a feeling of mastery of the art of managing, the respect of both your peers and your subordinates, and recognition as a manager who produces.

The roles reversed

Developing the delegation habit has made you aware of another aspect of your job: the fact that, in relation to your own boss, you are a delegatee. You are frequently assigned duties beyond your regular responsibilities. You are given opportunities to expand your horizons by tackling challenging tasks that your boss could have handled alone. You're participating in setting goals, being allowed to make decisions in new areas, receiving credit for broader accomplishments. Or are you?

By now, you know the advantages that can flow to you if your boss is a skilled delegator. Unfortunately, not all bosses are. Many face the same uncertainty, the same reluctance to give up control, the same guilt, fears, and anxieties that are described in earlier chapters. By now you know the stress that delegation can load on you. You know how hard it is to break old habits — the habit of being a 'doer', the habit of solving subordinates' problems for them, the habit of over-control. Your boss faces the same stresses and must deal with the same habits.

Being a good delegatee means more than just cooperating with your boss and conscientiously applying yourself to the tasks you are assigned. It is in your own interests and those of your organisation for you to take an active role in making your boss a better delegator. It might be easier to sit back and blame the confusion in your sector and your own mediocre results on your boss's inability to delegate, but your own career is on the line, too. You can't afford to sit on your hands. You have to take the offensive — without being offensive — to turn your boss into a more effective delegator.

Some guidelines are given below to help you become a more effective delegatee. You'll find that many of them are familiar because they're just the flip side of the principles that have guided you to being a solid delegator.

Talk about delegation

A frank discussion with your boss about the benefits and techniques of delegating, and about some of the obstacles that might stand in the way, is the best starting point. Then develop some convincing arguments to show that you're not trying to muscle in on his or her patch, but that delegation can help you both. Have at least one or two specific tasks in mind — like attending a meeting in your boss's place or preparing a report — that you think could be delegated to you immediately. Don't just talk in generalities. If your boss has failed to delegate to you in the past, show him or her why you're now ready to take on new duties. Don't harp on what you see as your boss's shortcomings. Rather, be positive about your own abilities.

Emphasise results

The increased time that delegation gives to your boss and the added experience it affords you are worth mentioning. But don't make them the heart of your argument. Remember that the ultimate goal of delegating is to attain results. Better results, greater productivity, more output; these are terms that every manager understands. Make sure your boss realises that results are your prime concern. If you talk about delegation as your stepping stone to a promotion, you may stir up feelings of envy or mistrust. Rather, empathise. Put yourself in his or her shoes.

Get involved

Perhaps your boss doesn't draw you into the decision-making process when assigning tasks. If you just sit quietly and listen, he or she may tell you outright what has to be done and how you are to do it. This is not an effective technique for delegating. By all means listen first and don't rudely interrupt. But counter this poor delegation technique by asking questions, involving yourself in setting goals, suggesting alternatives, and deciding on methods.

For example, your boss assigns you to consult with the engineers about alternative materials for the components you produce, and to file a report listing them. Your first question should be, What is the ultimate goal of the task, the results we want? What objective are we aiming at? Cost control? Preparation for material shortages? Improved product design? Inventory standardisation? Once you and your boss have settled on specific objectives, talk about how the report you are to prepare will contribute to them. You may be able to suggest ways of structuring the report that will make it more useful. If cost reduction is a goal, maybe a look at scrap values should be included. Participate. Try to make the task yours; don't just passively accept it as an assignment.

Aim for clarity

Your boss may not be an effective communicator. To avoid confusion and wasted effort later, make sure that the task, and particularly the goals of the task, are clear in your mind before you begin. Don't figure you'll play it by ear and go back to your boss for clarification every time a problem or unexpected development comes up. Solid delegation requires you to have a clear understanding of your responsibilities before you begin and not to run back to your boss unless a contingency develops outside the power you're given.

Insist on controls

'The boss said this project was my baby. He doesn't want to hear about it until it's signed, sealed, and delivered. I'm glad I won't have him breathing down my neck on this.' It's tempting to take the attitude that a lack of controls means freedom of action for you. But the smart delegatee insists on adequate controls. Why? Because a delegated task is usually an unfamiliar one. It may represent a substantial challenge to you. You may cruise along with confidence only to find that you've been driving up a dead-end road.

Controls protect you as much as they do your boss. You're the one who may be investing your time in a wasted effort. And you will probably be the one who will have to start over from scratch when something goes wrong. In addition, controls give you a clear idea of how your performance is going to be measured. Controls give you specific standards to shoot for. They make evaluation of your performance less of a judgement call.

If your boss doesn't suggest any control standards or checkpoints, suggest them yourself. If your boss says something vague like, 'Keep me posted on your progress,' you should offer to report at specific points during the project. Pay close attention to standards, progress reports, and deadlines even if your boss says they're optional. Remember, too, the value of self-controls. You may want to set up intermediate goals and standards to keep your own efforts on track.

Face up to delegation problems

Suppose you're given an assignment without the proper amount of authority or resources to carry it out. Or, you find that your area of responsibility on a delegated task overlaps with that of a colleague. Maybe control standards have been changed in midstream. Your boss fails to let you choose your own method on a delegated task. Or, you're doing all the work behind the scenes while your boss steals your applause. These, or any number of other delegation mistakes, indicate that your boss is not an ideal delegator. As a delegatee you should point out, diplomatically but persistently, how these faults are impairing the delegation process. Keep the discussion impersonal. Be positive and focus, as always, on the bigger and better results that both you and your boss could be achieving through more effective delegation.

Make your boss look good

Putting in a little extra effort on delegated assignments, completing tasks before the deadline, polishing a report, and double-checking for accuracy will all help build your boss's confidence in you. This can pay off in choicer delegations and more decision-making authority on future assignments. Certainly you deserve recognition for your work, but give your boss fair credit for the guidance and support that he or she has given you.

Give solutions, not problems

Don't hesitate to go to your boss for help or advice when you really need it. Taking on a task doesn't require you to climb out on a limb. But always try to avoid dumping problems in your boss's lap. Be especially careful if your boss is the type who grabs back delegated tasks at the first signs of trouble. Be frank but positive when discussing problems. Always have alternative solutions in mind before you present a problem to your boss. Depict difficulties in terms of options, not dilemmas. And remember that delegation does involve decision making on your part. Sometimes you should take a chance and try to find your own solution first before you involve your boss.

Keep your career goals in mind

One of your benefits as the delegatee is gaining experience in a variety of roles beyond your day-to-day duties. Your boss, however, may have you typecast. If you've done a good job in a task involving quality control, you may find yourself handed a series of delegated assignments in the same area. Your boss has confidence in your abilities and your name always comes to mind when a quality control project arises.

165

But maybe you need experience in production scheduling or materials planning. Don't hesitate to discuss this issue with your boss. Emphasise that you could do a better overall job if you had a more well-rounded view of the sector in which you work. Suggest some specific tasks that you would like to handle when the opportunity arises.

Passing on the delegation habit

The pinnacle of your performance as a delegator will be to pass on the delegation habit to your subordinates. The logic of this is clear: developing the managing skills of your people constitutes one of your main challenges as a manager. Nothing increases their effectiveness and productivity more than delegation. So while all your subordinates may not be in a position to learn good delegating habits, you shouldn't pass up any opportunities to engender those habits in your key people.

The first principle to get across to your subordinates is the law of comparative advantage. Remember that this rule states that work should be completed at the level where it can be accomplished with the greatest efficiency. That is, a secretary should type and an executive should manage, even though the executive may be an even faster typist. This idea will guide your subordinates to push work downwards in the organisation whenever possible, even though their own subordinates may take longer to complete it. It gets across the important concept that delegation is not an exercise in itself, not just a 'boss's prerogative', but a way for them to clear away routine tasks in order to make way for more productive work. The final goal is always increased results.

Second, you should emphasise controls. How to give over a task, let someone else make decisions, and yet still keep control constitutes the subtlest aspect of the art of delegation. Your people should try to master it from the beginning. Controls will encourage those subordinates who are too timid to pass along any task for which they have responsibility. Controls will make more careful those subordinates who think they can casually delegate and forget.

Getting started

An excellent way to introduce delegation to your people is

166

the team approach. Assign a particular project to a team and appoint a leader to direct the effort. Make it clear that you will hold that leader accountable for the outcome of the project, but that you expect him or her to make full use of the team members rather than take on the work alone. Suggest that the leader meet with each team member, set a specific subgoal, and delegate the tasks necessary to reach it, complete with controls.

This approach differs from a group or committee structure. While the concerted actions of the team members are important, what's more instructive to you and the leader is the way in which he or she parcels out accountability for the various phases of the project. You want to see whether the leader lets team members participate in setting objectives, establishes realistic deadlines, follows up on assignments, guides the work of the others without interfering, emphasises objectives over methods, and generally operates as a good delegator.

Setting an example

There is no better way to instill the delegation habit than to be an effective delegator yourself. Be consistent when you apply the techniques of delegation that you've learned. Delegate some tasks to each of your people. Delegate increasingly challenging ones to your key subordinates. Successful delegation is the best teacher of delegation.

When delegating, explain the process as you go along. Tell the delegatee why you are delegating, why you've chosen him or her, why you insist on controls, and why it's important that he or she participate in setting objectives. Always work towards getting the delegatee into the act, getting him or her involved in the process. The more input the person has in setting goals, defining the task, and establishing controls, the quicker that person will pick up the delegation habit and use it in his or her own managing.

New challenges for the delegator

The delegation habit makes you a better manager. Better yet, it's sure to make you an upwardly mobile one. Delegators are needed and wanted in the higher levels of management. They're versatile. They can take over a plant or a product line and immediately control their new positions. And they're productive. They know how to tap any company's most valuable resource: its people.

But promotions offer new challenges to the delegator. Your delegating style must change to meet the differing environments you meet as you move up the corporate ladder. The type of limited delegation suitable for a supervisor is hardly appropriate for a director. The following are some of the changing factors you will face as you climb the management pyramid.

What you delegate

Low-level delegators such as foremen and first-line supervisors usually keep a hand in all main aspects of their jobs. For example, a section supervisor may give a subordinate responsibility for a quality control study, but is unlikely to hand over total responsibility for quality control to another. Delegation at this level usually covers discrete, limited tasks.

At high management levels, delegations usually involve entire functions. While a plant manager has ultimate responsibility for worker health and safety, he or she may delegate that duty to a subordinate, asking only for periodic reports and statistics as controls. Such delegations are necessary because of the more substantial demands on high-level managers. A plant manager must establish priorities, delegating as completely as possible those areas not requiring his or her continuing attention.

How you delegate

The need to use skilful delegating techniques becomes even more vital at higher levels because the functions passed on to subordinates are themselves so comprehensive, complex, and important. No longer does a scrap report or a production scheduling assignment hang in the balance, but an entire marketing programme or an intricate research project. Offhand assignments, selection of the wrong delegatee, insufficient authority, failure to elicit subordinates' views — all these delegating errors have severe consequences for substantial delegations. That's why the ambitious manager should acquire a thorough grounding in delegation techniques early in his or her career.

The delegatee

Once above the supervisor level, you delegate almost entirely to subordinates who are also managing the efforts of other people. You will be calling not just on their personal efforts, but on the resources and people they have under their authority. This makes more critical their participation in setting objectives. Higher-level delegatees must be given wider latitude also to choose their own methods of operating. You are now farther removed from the actual circumstances of the task. That means you must rely much more on your delegatees and their people to make the right decisions needed for the assignment. The higher you get in management the more important it is to teach your subordinates to become delegators themselves. Only when all managers delegate well can your entire organisation reach peak effectiveness.

Controls

Delegation at higher levels requires refinement of controls. The plant manager who has delegated worker safety has neither the time nor the need to wade through weekly reports on all the various factors affecting safety. But at the same time, he has an absolute right and need to be informed of major accidents, serious health trends, or any significant new safety programmes. Proper controls should keep him informed on all of these topics, but must not burden him with extraneous details. Management by exception must be employed here. Exceptions must be targeted as the key factors in any delegated function. Selecting these factors, making controls lean but effective, and installing them at critical points are key to successful delegating at high management levels.

Forging ahead in business

Once you've learned to recognise these basic differences,

you won't worry much about how to delegate when you're established in your corner office in the executive suite. By then the delegation habit will be second nature to you. You'll have no difficulty adapting effective delegation techniques to any level of management.

Watch closely the styles of the top executives of well-run companies. You'll see how consistently they use effective delegating techniques. Don't jump to the conclusion that somehow becoming a top executive will turn you into an outstanding delegator. In fact, the reverse is true. It is effective delegation, the delegation habit, that has put those executives where they are — at the top.

Index